The first 40 YEARS

BY
Valerie Cox

ALONE

© ALONE

First published 2017

A catalogue record for this title is available from the British Library

ISBN 978-1-9997265-0-8

Printed in Ireland by Paceprint Ltd.

Cover Design by Bonfire

Page Layout by Artwerk Ltd.

CONTENTS

INTRODUCTION   7
ALONE – The First 40 Years

CHAPTER ONE: 11
Rolling Back The Clock – ALONE 1977-1999
– How It All Began

CHAPTER TWO: 45
The Nineties and Noughties – A New Era
– Keeping The Vision Alive

CHAPTER THREE: 51
The 2010's – ALONE Today – 'Strength In Unity' And Beyond
– A Conversation With Seán Moynihan

CHAPTER FOUR: 57
ALONE – An Organisation Of People

CHAPTER FIVE: 85
ALONE – And Campaigning – Changing Needs

CHAPTER SIX: 95
Concern for Older People – Yesterday to Today

CHAPTER SEVEN: 107
AlONE – Housing

CHAPTER EIGHT: 115
ALONE – The Good Times

CHAPTER NINE: 120
AND A NEW BEGINNING.

DEDICATION

The ALONE story is one of hundreds of unsung heroes who continue to volunteer, donate and work for ALONE. We express our deepest thanks to each and every one of you.

And to the thousands of older people whose lives we hope to have enriched, may you know how much you have enriched ours.

ABOUT THE AUTHOR

Giving a voice to the voiceless and telling the stories of ordinary people in both urban and rural Ireland has been at the core of Valerie Cox's many years working as a reporter and broadcaster. She spent over twenty years working on RTÉ radio programmes Morning Ireland, Drivetime and the Today Programme, bringing listeners stories of joy and sorrow, of happiness and loneliness, of crime and its effect on an older community. The issues she's tackled have been many — the problems of accessing the Fair Deal scheme, the closure of rural Garda Stations and Post Offices, the lack of end -of-life facilities and caring for older people in the community— and she has taken up the cudgel on behalf of those in danger of losing their homes.

Valerie has worked with ALONE on a number of occasions, meeting some of the people who are at the heart of this book: the older people they support and their volunteers. She is the author of three previous books, Searching, which tells the story of Ireland's missing people, The Family Courts and A Ploughing People. She is also a Patron of Wicklow Hospice.

Valerie lives in rural Wicklow with her husband Brian, and the couple have five children and four grandchildren.

FOREWARD

The year 1977 was a significant year for many reasons - Peace People founders Mairead Corrigan and Betty Williams received a Nobel Prize for Peace, the first of the hugely successful 'Star Wars' movies opened, Queen Elizabeth celebrated 25 years on the throne and another member of royalty - the 'King' - Elvis Presley died.

Amongst these headlines emerged the story of a Dublin firefighter, Willie Bermingham, who set up the charity ALONE (A Little Offering Never Ends). In 1977, Willie had been working at Tara Street Fire Station for 13 years and, during this time, had become appalled by the plight of the forgotten old, many of whom he discovered having died of neglect and in abject poverty. Along with some colleagues in Tara Street, he decided to take action and make a difference to the lives of older people all over Dublin. It was his unwavering dedication to both fire fighting and ALONE that earned him the title of 'International Firefighter of the Year' in 1985.

This book beautifully chronicles the evolution of ALONE from its humble origins in 1977 to today and showcases the groundbreaking work the charity has done and continues to do to support older people in Ireland. Valerie Cox and the team at ALONE have done a fantastic job in producing a book that can teach all citizens, young and old, the importance of humanity and reaching out to the more vulnerable members of our society.

There have been many changes over the past 40 years - people are living longer, there are more extensive and accessible supports and there have been significant advances in health care reforms. However, older people in Ireland are still affected by loneliness and isolation. In Dublin Fire Brigade we continue to hear stories of older people living in near squalor conditions with limited family support and often lacking the riches that companionship and social networks can bring. I frequently hear stories where our firefighters bring older people into hospital and worry about what happens to them when they return home, or if they get to go home at all.

ALONE is as important now as it was in 1977. The work the charity does today reflects Willie's ethos of compassion and a person-centred approach. In the Dublin Fire Brigade, we are happy to be entering this year into a formal partnership with ALONE supporting them to help older people age at home.

Patrick Fleming
Chief Fire Officer
Dublin Fire Brigade

INTRODUCTION
ALONE – THE FIRST 40 YEARS

Willie Bermingham at Tara Street Fire Station in the 1970s

It was 1977 and the bodies of three older people lay undiscovered in their homes in Dublin for several weeks. A young fireman, Willie Bermingham, who had retrieved one of the bodies, decided to bring some humanity to older people living and dying on their own. So, he gave up a packet of cigarettes a day and spent the money printing posters, which he distributed around the city.

That's how simple it was – ALONE was born.

Willie organised volunteers to visit those living alone. Later, he built a housing scheme. Today, forty years later, ALONE is still looking after those whom society has ignored and forgotten. The homeless are housed, the lonely are visited, and the dead are given a decent burial in the Millennium Plot in Glasnevin Cemetery.

This book tells the story of ALONE, from its humble origins in 1977, responding to the need that young fireman saw then, to what it has become today. This book is a tribute to the organisation started by Willie Bermingham, who died so tragically young aged 48 in April 1990, and by the group of people who responded to the raw need of older

Willie Bermingham with Bertie Ahern, Lord Mayor of Dublin, in 1986

people in the Dublin of the seventies. It is a tribute to the thousands of volunteers and others who in the past 40 years have not forgotten the older people who fall through society's safety nets. In a sense, what Willie Bermingham started in 1977 is the safety net for these older people.

Forty years later, ALONE is stronger than ever. Its ethos has never changed. Its priority has always been the welfare of isolated and lonely older people who find themselves on the margins of society. Its Mission is simple – ALONE supports older people to age at home. This book looks at the changes over the years, the campaigns being fought and won, the stance that has been taken by ALONE against government cutbacks, landlords and bureaucracy and the small army of volunteers who support older people.

Today, ALONE is an organisation that supports over 1,000 older people a year, has 100 units of Housing with Support, 500+ (and growing) Befriending Volunteers, in addition to Support Coordinators, Telephone Befriending Services, and events and activities. An organisation that has started to deliver services outside Dublin County, into the Northeast of the country, it also coordinates a network of befriending services across the country in Befriending Network Ireland.

ALONE is also at the forefront of developing new technologies to improve how services can be coordinated, developing apps and management information systems (MIS) that can be used by other organisations. These technologies will enable the wider sector of older people agencies to gather valuable data on the extent of the issues facing older people and the contributions these agencies (not only ALONE) provide to help older people to age at home.

Times have certainly changed. However, the tragedy is that ALONE is needed now as much as ever, responding to a different type of poverty in a fast and forgetful world. After forty years, there is cause for celebration – a celebration of the strength and decency of Ireland's older people and of the kindness, tenacity and love of the volunteers. Ireland is indeed a better place because of organisations like ALONE who never forget the isolated and the lonely.

CHAPTER ONE:
ROLLING BACK THE CLOCK
ALONE 1977-1999 - HOW IT ALL BEGAN

'It all started over a pint of Guinness with Willie!' That's how Pat Morgan recalls the birth of ALONE. Pat was the manager of the Bank "They won't take my signature, would you sign something for me?" asked Willie.

"I will of course',' I said, what else could I say?"

Willie was asking Pat to sign the documents required to form a 'Friendly Society' to be known as ALONE – 'A Little Offering Never Ends.' Pat wasn't the 'hands on' person – that was obviously Willie – but 'Willie was a fireman and they wouldn't take his signature – if you worked in a bank, they thought you must be really trustworthy. The stupidity of the times!'

Pat met Willie once a month. 'Someday we'll have lunch,' we'd say, 'but we never got round to it. I knew Willie, I trusted him.' But, ironically, it was Pat who became very much the 'hands-on' person as ALONE progressed.

Things got complicated when the Registrar for Friendly Societies sent back Willie's Book of Rules, because they wanted certain changes. Willie corrected them and sent them back, but they were returned again. 'Willie got very annoyed and threw the whole bloody lot down. "I'm not going to do it – forget it!" he said.

So, that's how, without any formal structure, Willie Bermingham started ALONE. Following this, however, he began to buy properties to house their 'guests.' It was then that he realised he needed to create a legal entity. Some of those early properties were purchased in the names of Willie and Pat Morgan. A Dublin solicitor, David Turner, also became involved with the organisation. Willie had gone to David for advice when he was arguing with the landlords of some of the older people he was looking out for. Pat's brother, Tom Morgan, a barrister, also acted for ALONE.

Even for an infant organisation, accounts were always kept and audited. The archives carry details of everything that was ever spent. All donations were documented meticulously. The first year's accounts were produced in December 1977. The auditor's report was signed off by Chartered Accountants Vincent P. Lynch and Anthony Dowling.

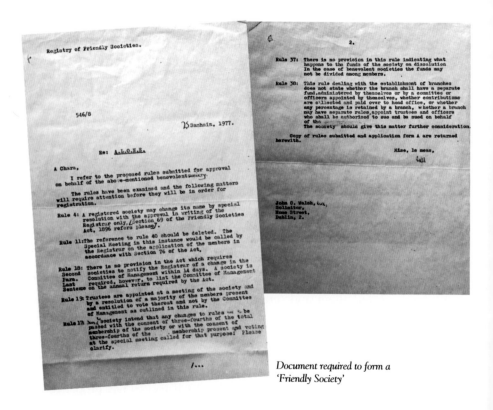

Document required to form a 'Friendly Society'

Donations totalled £2,320 (the equivalent of €15,275 today). Bank charges were £1. There were 49 members, each of whom paid £1 to join.

1977, however, also saw a bank strike. In the middle of it, Willie's phone was cut off. According to Pat Morgan, 'He got so angry he got a coffin lid and wrote a cheque to the Post Office. He threw it at them, saying "People will die because you bloody well cut off my phone'!' Even though the phone was in Willie's home, it was used for ALONE so that people could phone in emergencies. Morgan says he still recalls a porter walking out with the coffin lid. Later it became a fixture on the wall of a shed in Willie's garden. And, yes, the post office did put the cheque through the system!

Willie also demonstrated his ire with authority when the Minister for Social Welfare sent a cheque to help the work. Willie sent it back! This was an important gesture from Willie, signalling that he wasn't satisfied with handouts, and that he wanted the Government to start looking after the older population, instead of seeing it as a job for charity. His sister Patricia says, 'ALONE is his legacy but he didn't mean for ALONE to continue. He wanted the government to take over looking after the older people. It's the older people of Ireland who built Ireland to what it is, and for the Government and Health Boards to look after older people and leave them with dignity, that was his aim and for ALONE to disband. That's what he always said to me when we'd be having our little bevvies in the Cottage Inn! But it hasn't happened and it's never going to happen at the rate it's going now.' Patricia believes that in twenty years' time, there will be more squalor than there was in the middle of the last century.

The first Annual General Meeting of ALONE was held at 8.30p.m. on 15th February 1978 in Wynn's Hotel in Lower Abbey Street. The Patrons were Charles J. Haughey and Dr John F O'Connell. But the real genesis of ALONE began two years earlier when Willie Bermingham, the fireman, attended the scene of several horrific cases of older people dying in appalling poverty or living in cold, wet, hungry, lonely conditions, all in the country's capital city. Perhaps the catalyst was the discovery of the body of an old man who had died alone and in squalor in Charlemont Street. He had been dead for a number of weeks before the Fire Brigade had been called. They broke into the flat to find rats gnawing at the man's body. Over the next few weeks eight older people were found dead in their homes. Willie sprang into action, and printed and distributed 200 posters highlighting what had happened.

The early years of ALONE were a family affair. Willie's wife, Marie, and their five children were all co-opted as volunteers, and as Willie didn't drive, Marie ('the cook' as he called her) drove him everywhere. Willie's colleagues in Dublin Fire Brigade, all witnesses to the neglect and horrific conditions for many older people in Dublin, rowed in behind him. Meetings were held in all kinds of places, including Willie's yard and the family kitchen.

It was a tough time for many Dubliners. Kevin McConville, one of the first volunteers, describes the city at the time as having grown 'old and ugly.' The demolition of the inner city had started and thousands of people were moved out to the wild delights of Tallaght and Clondalkin, leaving many older people to cope alone. People were led to believe that television was "the pagan in the corner" as Eamon de Valera had described it. Many thought that television was great company but found that it was a poor substitute for interaction with friends and neighbours. People knew what was going on and tut-tutted but Willie Bermingham was the one who did something about it.

WILLIE – THE EARLY YEARS
To understand the kind of person Willie was, we need to go back to the roots of the Bermingham family. His Dad, William, hailed from Narranmore in Co Kildare. When William was only ten years old, his father was killed in a farm accident. So William, the eldest of

seven children, became the breadwinner for his family. Willie's sister, Patricia, tells the story that her grandmother, Bridget, was expecting a baby, the youngest Lizzy, when her husband died. Times were hard and, as Patricia puts it, 'even in those days the banks were in power.' The family had a mortgage on their farm and the bank took it over, sold off their stock and they were evicted from their home.

Eventually, Bridget's brother, Jim, packed them all up and took them to live in Dublin where he got them a cottage in The Puck in Inchicore. They had a good life there. William Snr met Marie Kelly and married in 1937. Stephen was born in 1939, followed by Bernie in 1941 and Willie in 1942. Patricia, the baby, was born in the fifties. Their father bought a smallholding in Bluebell and started off rearing pigs, horses and hens. At one time, he had 200 cattle, (which he grazed in the Phoenix Park), and 150 pigs. They cut turf on the Dublin Mountains and reared turkeys for Christmas. Their father was a hard worker who only slept five hours a night. He rented land from Nugget shoe polish.

Willie Bermingham & family

As a kid, Willie was generous beyond his years. In the late fifties he took it upon himself to start helping their older neighbours. One of these projects didn't go down too well with his father when he discovered that Willie had been collecting the farm eggs and giving them away to their older neighbours. Says Patricia, 'Our mother was as bad as he was!'

The Dublin of the fifties saw terrible poverty. Willie and his brother Stephen would go out with a load of coal and turf and logs, 'but regularly Willie would return with no money. He'd be giving the stuff on credit, he was always in trouble with my father.'

Willie Bermingham as a child

Willie and his Mam became very involved with those who were poor and lonely in their own area. Patricia remembers the death of one older lady. Willie used to visit her and bring her eggs. He was about 12 years old and he couldn't get an answer one day, so he looked in the window, but couldn't see her. Her dogs were howling. He told his mother and she got into the house and found the old lady dead. The rats were eating her body and her dogs were exhausted from trying to protect her by killing the rats. The neighbours paid for her funeral.

Then there was a woman they called 'Tizzy.' 'To us she was very old, small and wizened and suffered from arthritis. She lived in very poor conditions, there were no floorboards in her house, just a clay floor and rags for curtains. On Saturday evenings Mam would bring her in for her tea.'

As a young man, Willie had various jobs. He sold fuel, worked as a bouncer in the local pub, and became quite an entrepreneur with his singing cousins. Then there was a spell working as a gravedigger in the Bluebell and Esker cemeteries.

The family was very proud when Willie joined the Dublin Fire Brigade. The first Christmas, however, he was on night duty. There was a tragic fire overnight and a young family was burnt to death. He came into the house on Christmas morning smelling of burnt flesh. 'He was upset, heartbroken, he had carried out the remains of the family.'

In 1977, he found an old man dead, having collapsed under the stairs while trying to put a shilling in his gas meter. His body wasn't found for a long time. He was covered in bluebottles as the body had started to decay. Patricia says that was the real start of ALONE. Willie had posters made up and he stuck them up in shops and churches. Willie also got his sister to buy him a Sweeps ticket every week but he never won. His *nom de plume* was 'ALONE' but she never knew what it stood for.

At this point, Patricia was expecting her fourth child. She remembers she was making apple tarts one day when Willie came into the house and said he had been down in a church and the sky pilot (the Parish Priest) wouldn't let him put up his posters for ALONE in the church porch. He was so upset that tears welled up in his eyes.

Willie never drove a car. His wife, Marie, drove him everywhere. But in the sixties, Willie did drive an NSU motorbike. Patricia tells the story of Willie's trip to the dentist when he had all his teeth taken out. He was to be one of the best men at her wedding and she warned him he'd better have those teeth in for the wedding. 'On the morning, he went off to collect the teeth but coming along the Naas road on his bike, the teeth were hurting him, he stopped the bike, took them out and threw them into a field and never wore a set of teeth again!'

*ALONE 'Search that
building campaign 1977'*

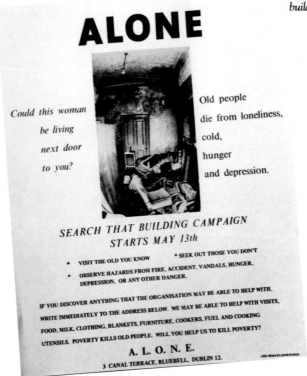

ALONE – A LEGACY TO A MAN AND HIS VISION

ALONE has become Willie Bermingham's legacy, but, as Patricia explained, he didn't intend that ALONE would continue. He felt the government should take over its responsibility for looking after Ireland's older people, the people who built Ireland. He was adamant that it was the government and the Health Boards who should look after older people and leave them with their dignity. That was his aim. When that time came, he would disband ALONE. History, however, tells the rest of the story. The Government didn't step up to the mark and ALONE was never disbanded. Its focus may have changed, but it is true to say that as an organisation, it is needed today more than ever.

Willie may not be happy with this scenario; that ALONE is still providing such an essential service, 40 years after its foundation. Willie also believed that ALONE should be a completely voluntary organisation, but as his sister Patricia says, 'times have changed and he might have changed as time went on.' She believes that if Willie had lived, then ALONE wouldn't exist today, that the government would be doing their job. 'If he had lived, he would have forced the government to take care of older people and he took no nonsense from them. He would apologise to no-one for the language he used, he was straight to the point, no bullshit!'

Willie Bermingham
– Derek Speirs Photography

The tragedy of the story, of course, is that Willie died aged 47. He had been sick for two years beforehand. But despite the severity of his illness, he was determined to throw a party for his mother's 81st birthday. 'Even if I'm in the coffin myself, I'll give her a party!' he said. After Willie's death, Marie (his wife) and Liam O'Cuanaigh, Administrator, decided to carry on and run the organisation themselves. But it was a turbulent time, there were frictions and both Marie and Liam ended up resigning as Trustees and walking away from it all.

In a letter dated 29th April 1992, Marie Bermingham officially resigned as Chairperson and Trustee of ALONE. Kevin McConville, who was also a trustee, says he and fellow trustee, Kevin Kelleher, knew nothing about their decision in advance, and only found out when they turned up to hear the announcement at a meeting on Saturday April 23rd, along with the media.

'Resignation stuns ALONE!' said the Evening Press, where Sile Yeats reported that Marie Bermingham told the hushed meeting that she was very sad to be leaving. Mr O'Cuanaigh told the meeting that he could not continue in ALONE if Marie Bermingham felt she had to leave. Mrs. Bermingham was close to tears, wrote Yeats, saying she was too upset to discuss the crisis. 'It's heart-breaking,' she told the Evening Press, 'and it's a terrible thing to have happened. ALONE is not the organisation that Willie founded. It has changed in the last two years, and I feel there is no place for me in it.'

Journalist Ed O'Loughlin reported that the reason behind Marie Bermingham's resignation were 'disagreements over a bequest and over general matters of style and direction.'

Kevin McConville says they then held a meeting of the trustees, 'we needed someone to take the helm as soon as possible.' They knew of a ship's Captain, Harry Sheill, who was home from sea at the time and he agreed to give it his best shot. Kevin McConville says it was 'the force of Harry's decency that kept people together, that kept the organisation running.'

THE ARCHIVES
cases at this time

housing conditions in the 1970s and 1980s
...ublin – Derek Speirs photography

ALONE

The vagaries of Irish weather, in which four seasons can be experienced in just a single day, affect the old and the poor more than anyone else. Since its foundation, ALONE has campaigned to provide heating and fuel for older people, and has encouraged neighbours to watch out for them especially during harsh winters and cold spells.

'Cold blamed for deaths of two women,' said the Irish Times headline on 4th January 1979. Paul Murray described the electric wiring in a house on the North Circular Road as 'so decayed it could not be used – the only light was a small oil lamp.' Off the South Circular Road, Murray says another lady, aged 70, was found dead on Tuesday. 'She had been dead for about seven days. Her Christmas turkey, cake and pudding lay untouched. She had been last seen by neighbours a day or two after Christmas Day.'

Writing in Hibernia on 3rd May 1979, Máirín de Búrca described some of the cases being dealt with by ALONE and asked: How can this problem be tackled? 'Well, for one thing, it is a relatively small problem,' she wrote, 'taking 250 as the figure for the size of the problem it should not be beyond the ingenuity of a modern city, with a population of some 800,000 people to deal with.'

'Many old people living alone in Dublin dread the winter to come,' said the November/December ALONE newsletter in 1984, 'a winter that will see some die from cold, crime, loneliness, hopelessness and depression. Already in Dublin, one 64 year old woman has died from malnutrition, and her 70 year old husband saved just in the nick of time.'

Long, cold, dark nights leave hundreds of older people in great danger. Hypothermia, freezing to death, is a real risk when body temperature drops even a few degrees. Darkness gives cover to thugs and vandals and enables some unscrupulous landlords to use 'dirty trick' tactics to have older tenants evicted.

'Use of open fires and unreliable heaters brings the hazards of fires, scalding and other accidents. Many older people without electricity resort to candle light – a practice that saw two older women incinerated in a Phibsborough flat last winter.

'Severe weather will see many old folk trapped indoors without proper meals or human company – leading to self-neglect and great depths of depression. An example of the vulnerability of the old came as recently as October 27th last, when an older Dublin couple were taken to hospital in the middle of the night. They lived in a small, desolate, Corporation flat off Whitefriar Street which later showed signs of a desperate existence.'

The woman died in hospital, officially from a bone marrow disease, but behind this tactful explanation lay the fact that she was in an extreme state of malnutrition. The husband resigned himself to the fact that his wife would go into a pauper's grave. However, arrangements were made by ALONE to give her a dignified funeral in Co Wicklow.'

In September/October 1987, the ALONE News Bulletin again focused on the weather with a collection of horror stories. And, according to ALONE, these events unfolded as officialdom couldn't make up its mind about a special Task Force for 'the beleaguered old.' It had been discussed since 1979.

'Another dreadful year'…said the headline on the ALONE News Bulletin and it went on to list a number of appalling cases:

- A 74 year old widow with a history of stomach disease froze to death in a rat-infested basement on North Circular Road. Her special-needs 50 year old son was to die in the same conditions a year later.
- An older woman in Gardiner Street burned to death after falling into a coal fire on which she tried to boil potatoes.
- In Fairview, a widow of 87 died in a rain-soaked house, which

had been sabotaged by a landlord in a six year campaign to drive her out.

- An older brother and sister were trapped in a cold, damp basement flat in Mount Street.
- A man in his seventies was living in a roofless cottage in Drumcondra without toilet, electricity or cooking facilities.
- A man in his early sixties was living in a fire damaged flat in Ballsbridge amid mounds of papers, trash, rotten food and surrounded by his favourite 'friends' – hundreds of tropical fish...almost all of them dead.
- A savage dog kept neighbours at bay at a 'haunted house' in Phibsborough where an old man died in cold and filth.
- On South Circular Road an old widow was found dead on New Year's Day, her Christmas hamper unopened.

MARCH 1979 – Highlighting the horrific living conditions of older people living alone in Dublin
To highlight the dire living conditions in Dublin at the time, ALONE issued a press release detailing a number of harrowing case studies of neglected older people who were 'just now emerging from what must have been one of the most cruel winters of their lives.'

The charity said that a combination of electricity and postal strikes, the collapse of the free turf scheme, and damage to buildings due to the cold and flooding 'amounted to little less than private execution.'
It gave the example of 'at least two old women who died in extremely cold conditions around Christmas.' One was found after a week and had not even opened a Christmas hamper, while the other, a 76-year-old, was discovered in freezing conditions in a rat-infested basement.

The charity also details the gruesome story of a woman living alone who was burned to death on the open fire she resorted to in order to cook 'a small meal of potatoes.'

As ALONE tells it, the situation was no better for older men living alone: 'Among the cases brought to our notice in the past month were: A bachelor of 72 in the north city suburbs who has raw ulcers from the feet up to the knees, who is unable even to dress himself in a house without water, toilet or cooking facilities, who lives with the smell of human excrement and the carcasses of dead cats, and who is in desperate need of hospitalisation.'

The organisation points out its volunteer members are dealing with 'dozens of cases of this type,' and summarises the plight of older people living alone in clinical fashion: 'It's also said that one cigarette takes a few minutes off a human life. If this is true, some of the old people we have discovered could be better advised to smoke a hundred cigarettes a day to put a quicker end to their misery.'

MARCH 1984

Five years later, and the living conditions of many older people in the capital showed no improvement.

In March 1984, two women were killed in a flatland fire in Dublin. It is believed that one of the women had been lighting candles, and this led to the blaze.

One of the women was known to ALONE, and Willie Bermingham issued a statement following the tragedy to highlight in particular the difficulty older women had living alone.

He told of a 70-year-old woman the charity discovered was living in an attic flat on Ormond Quay. She lived without proper sanitary facilities, and had to climb 64 steps to her 'cold isolated room.' She protected her meat stuffs from rats by suspending the food in plastic bags on a string running from wall to wall.

However, as Willie explains in this statement, some lonely older people were so desperate for company they welcomed the rats: 'About a month ago we met a man in Ranelagh whose dilapidated cottage is held up at one corner by a wardrobe. He is ill and in his late fifties and is so lonely betimes that he makes up dinners for the rats who gather in the 200-year-old shack.'

Willie concludes by pointing out 'these are just a few sad cases, but they are not sensational.'

ALONE AGM – March 31, 1985

At the organisation's AGM in March 1985, Willie Bermingham said that brutality against the 'helpless old' was the most frightening feature of the plight of old people living alone in Dublin.

Willie said every week 'brought distress calls from neighbours, distant relations, Gardaí, fire brigade, social workers, tradesmen, meter readers and the like about isolated old people in need of protection.'

He said the main issues old people living alone were dealing with at that stage were squalid living conditions, rent arrears, the threat of eviction, and illness.

He pointed out that 'at least' six people were found dead after prolonged periods, giving the example of Parnell St where a man in his seventies was discovered after three months, his body 'greatly decayed.'

In another case in the northern inner city, a man was found to have been preyed on for weeks by vermin and his own household pets.

At the AGM, the ALONE chief also bemoaned the dismantling of the Rent Restrictions Act – which limited tenant rights – saying it had caused distress to the 'rent-burdened old.'

He tells of the eviction of a 78-year-old man from this lifelong home in Grattan St, which was thankfully reversed following a joint campaign from ALONE and Threshold.

Willie was critical of Dublin Corporation's role in dealing with older people who were behind on their rent, saying notices to quit were served to older people renting, over arrears of as little as £14.

1984 also brought, for what ALONE described as 'reasons unknown,' a rise in the number of older people discharged from hospitals into unfit and unsanitary conditions.

Willie highlights the cases of an 80-year-old man who was sent home from James Connolly Hospital by taxi at 4am to "poor conditions," and a Donegal woman in her 70s who was discharged from hospital, came to Dublin in distress, was sent home and died in Donegal just three days later.

At the AGM, the organisation describes as its 'most significant event' of the year the purchase of a half-acre site in Artane where eight cottage-type dwellings were planned.

Although full planning permission was still sought, Willie Bermingham said 'With luck, some homeless may be fixed up before Christmas next.'

The charity also bought seven small dwellings across the city that year to accommodate the 'desperate elderly,' bringing the total to 20.

Willie concluded his address to the AGM by pointing out that ALONE's property dealings were all covered by an accumulating reserve fund and "thanks to the unsolicited donations of well-wishers".

He added the organisation would regularly spurn 'many offers of fundraising that involved gimmickry, exploitation of misfortune among the old, or profiteering by the so called fundraisers.'

'I feel I'm a square peg in a round hole'

The charity regularly receives requests for assistance from desperate older people who feel they have no place else to turn.

In the modern technological era, being heard has never been easier, but it was not always like that.

Over the years, particularly in the early days, ALONE would have received a plethora of letters from older people as a cry for help in desperate circumstances.

One letter, written by 'Thomas' in the 1990s, typifies the gap ALONE filled in essential services. He asks if he can be considered for a one-bed flat in Willie Bermingham House in Kilmainham. Thomas explains that he has been homeless since the death of his father. His family decided to sell the family home, with the proceeds divided seven ways. He says he then moved to a flat in Rathmines with a rent of £19 a week, but the landlord raised this to £32 after 'a few weeks.' Thomas explains his share of the family home was 'swallowed up in rent' and his brothers and sisters would not take 'a diabetic burden into their homes.' As a result he was made homeless for a period, before securing a cheap flat with his pension. However, he could not settle there, due to the 'coming and going all night' of cars. The flat also became flooded from the flat above, leading to Thomas spending 12 weeks in hospital with pneumonia. He begs for ALONE to consider his application for somewhere to live and desperately stresses: 'I feel I'm a square peg in a round hole.'

ALONE and the end of THE PAUPER'S GRAVE

1988 was a memorable year for ALONE – it was the year when pauper's graves came to an end, and it was the year when Willie Bermingham received an honorary doctorate from Trinity College, Dublin.

There had always been a problem when older people died alone in poverty. They rarely had papers for a family grave and, indeed, many had totally lost that family connection years earlier. The practice was that older people who died with nothing were buried in a pauper's grave with no headstone. This enraged Willie, as did his negotiations

ALONE's Millenium Plot

with a certain Catholic priest who refused to hold a funeral service for an old man who died, on the basis that they didn't know whether he was Catholic or not.

However, Willie found an ally in Dean Victor Griffen of St Patrick's Cathedral who was happy to carry out the necessary services as they arose. Sometimes there might have been only three or four people at one of these funerals. The Dean was very welcoming to everyone, regardless of religious belief.

The genesis of the Millennium Plot goes back to 1984, when Willie was at a funeral in Glasnevin cemetery and he saw a wooden box on a wheelbarrow. When he asked about it he was told that this was somebody who had nobody to bury them, and it was bound for a 'pauper's grave.' This meant burial in an unmarked piece of ground between the other graves.

ALONE News Bulletin 1988

Willie Bermingham receiving honorary doctorate degree

As recorded in a 1984 ALONE newsletter, Willie swore from then on that nobody would ever be buried an unmarked grave again. ALONE then oversaw the burials of those who had died without family or friends, were unidentified, unclaimed or homeless.

At the ALONE AGM in March 1985, it was pointed out that 'simple funeral costs' of between £700 and £1,000 would mean 'the penniless elderly can't expect a rush to their deathbeds of remote relatives who will be landed with the bills.' Difficulties around the cost of funerals and a respectful send-off for older people living alone who had died was also raised. The charity said that, in the previous year, it had to "bury, or finance in part the funerals, of eight people who would otherwise have been dropped into pauper's graves".

The breakthrough came in 1988 in Dublin's Millennium year when ALONE secured a plot from Glasnevin – The Millennium Plot. The September/October ALONE News Bulletin reported that the stigma of a pauper's graves was to end as the 'Corporation accepts use of 'ALONE' Millennium Plot.' 'No More Pauper Graves' was the theme adopted by ALONE for the Millennium Year in an attempt to eradicate from Ireland's capital city, of the dire practise of dropping the poor into unmarked 'poor ground' graves.

On October 28th, it read, the campaign should be declared a success as Dublin Corporation have now, de facto, accepted the use of ALONE's Millennium burial plot at Glasnevin Cemetery. 'Nine people who might otherwise have been relegated to the pauper's section have already been buried in the new Plot in 1988.'

Inside, the Bulletin commented that 'the very existence of these plots is an affront to the dignity of the people of the capital city, and is a real source of dread to many old folk eking out their last years in loneliness and poverty.' It is known that some old people forsake medical care, proper heat and nutrition out of great fear of being dumped into a lonely, unmarked pauper's grave. The number of such squalid burials (which sometimes take place without the body even being taken to a church) has in fact dropped in recent years – but mainly because various voluntary groups and hostels have intervened to give the destitute dead a respectful send off.'

The Bulletin went on to report that ALONE had already conducted five burials at the new site and had overseen four others in the Millennium Year, 'pointing up the stark reality of poverty and death in Dublin in 1988.' These burials included an unidentified body found in a quarry. There was great kindness shown in making the Plot the best it could be.

Every person who is laid to rest in the plot has their burial marked with their name inscribed on a headstone. Sometimes people come to the plot looking for the name of a family member who has gone missing and they take some comfort from the knowledge that that person was treated with dignity in death.

Some guests of ALONE choose to have their last resting place in the Millennium Plot, happy that they are being laid to rest by friends and among friends. The restoration of the Plot in time for the 35th anniversary of ALONE in 2012 was part-funded by the Ireland Funds. At a ceremony in Glasnevin on July 25th that year, ALONE CEO Seán Moynihan said, 'Many good friends have passed away over the 35 years. Our hope is that our work and memories keep them alive, as we believe each and every person's story is unique and should be valued and remembered today.'

A plaque was unveiled by Senator David Norris and the then Chairman of ALONE, Pat Morgan, paid tribute to Willie's very supportive family, led by his wife Marie, and the great volunteers who surrounded Willie. 'He only wanted volunteers who would be prepared to do everything he did himself – and he baulked at nothing,' said Pat. He went on to say that Ireland has moved on since the foundation of ALONE. 'Many of the things fought for are now part of Government policy, for example Home Helps, Day Care Centres, tenants' rights. Landlords are no longer all-powerful. Organisations have been established to look after the interests of older people; but unfortunately, there are still people and situations that fall through the net. This is where ALONE steps in and takes care of those most in need, in crisis circumstances and in a non-judgemental way.'

Kevin McConville recalled that members of the public donated grave plots to ALONE so that they could be used instead of pauper's graves. The offers of graves were taken up, and many older people were laid to rest with complete strangers through the great kindness of the families involved. In some cases the graves had just one or two spaces left and the donors knew they wouldn't be used again.

Pat was adamant that ALONE would not have survived to 35 years were it not for four things, 'Our loyal trustees; the voluntary unsolicited financial contributions by the public; the loyalty and dedication of our administrators over the years, Liam O'Cuanaigh, Harry Sheill, Pat Lane and our present CEO Seán Moynihan and his trusted staff; and finally, and most important of all, the wonderful and dedicated volunteers, hundreds and hundreds over the years who give of their time, energy and commitment and who bring companionship, friendship and fun to our wonderful elderly guests.'

FROM THE ARCHIVES

This is a flavour of the Minutes of ALONE meetings from 1984-1997

The meeting dealt with a man who had been evicted from a guest house and who was now in Leopardstown hospital because no emergency accommodation was available after he was discharged from the Mater hospital. Willie Bermingham decided to take him to his own home and to care for him until they found something suitable for him. Two further evictions were discussed, with one of the men involved now living in a caravan. A video of one of the evictions was produced and this was later screened in Deansgrange Library and in Maynooth College.

There were problems with a man who had died, as his relatives could not be found. ALONE agreed to bear the cost of the burial, which was £400.

An old man living in York Street flats had died. His flat had been on the top floor and he had to climb 69 steps from the street to the flat.

An older lady had been found unconscious in her flat on Clontarf Road. There was a report of the death of an old man they visited and they heard that the Task Force was carrying out work on a house in Glasnevin.

A house had been destroyed by fire in Ranelagh, it would cost £40,000 to rebuild. There was an eviction from a flat in Manor Street. An old lady had died and left her clothing and furniture to ALONE in her will. An old lady had left Dublin and returned to her relations in Ballinasloe and was said to be 'very happy.'

The Task Force reported that Miss B's house was in 'too bad a state to clear,' and would cost £3,000. Another pensioner had a gas bill with £700 arrears, and ALONE was in contact with the Gas Company. It was reported that an old man had been found dead in his flat in Parnell Street. His body had been there for approximately ten weeks before being discovered. He had been living in terrible conditions and 'while dead, rats had been feeding from his body.

It was reported that a 93 year old woman had died. She had been the victim of a burglary, and had never recovered from the ordeal of the break in.'

The committee arranged for an old lady's funeral. Her local Church of Ireland had refused to hold it, so they arranged for it to go ahead in the Church of the Holy Trinity, Rathmines.

The meeting organised contact with Meals on Wheels for some of their guests. They also reported the purchase of ALONE's fourteenth house at Irwin Terrace, East Wall, for £10,000.

A call was received from a guest house owner to say a taxi had left an old woman at the guest house in Palmerstown and they had no room for her. Willie Bermingham checked her into a hotel for the night and met her the following morning when he came off night duty. It turned out that she was 69 and had been discharged from a hospital in Co Donegal the previous day. She went to another hospital, again in Donegal. However, she was told she was not ill enough to be admitted. So, she got a lift to Leitrim but missed the train to Dublin. She then got a taxi and used all her money on the fare. The woman was from Donegal and the Gardai were involved in getting in touch with her local garda station. She agreed to return to Donegal. At 11:15 p.m. that night Willie got a phone call to say she was home and safe.

An old man had been taken into Garda custody for knocking on a door. ALONE went to his rescue. Then, an 84 year old woman was evicted from a Corporation flat in Dolphin's Barn. However, it was claimed that the woman had not lived there for three years and the flat was occupied by her granddaughter and two young men. There had been complaints from neighbours. Willie Bermingham agreed with the Corporation's action in this case.

There was an urgent call to the office to say that an old woman was sitting on a chair on the Oath in Ranelagh. She appeared to be cold and dejected and had all her belongings beside her on the path. The concern was that she had been evicted. Willie Bermingham went to investigate immediately, only to discover that she was a flower seller waiting on a delivery of flowers from the markets!

The body of an older man from Devitt House had been found in the canal. The meeting had an update on another older man who had been injured in a break in into his house in May.

Willie Bermingham had received a phone call to say that the wife of a couple admitted to Dr Stephen's hospital suffering from malnutrition had died.

Willie also reported on attending court for a man who had received an eviction notice due to £70 arrears on his rent. ALONE paid it off and the case was struck out.

Another guest had died and had no life insurance so ALONE paid for the funeral.

Relatives could not be found for a man who had died in the Hospice, so it was arranged that he would be buried in the ALONE grave in Mount Jerome cemetery.

Two more cases of malnutrition were reported from Bray, Co Wicklow.

ALONE had to notify the Fire Brigade to enter a house where an old lady was found dead. She had been dead for several days when they found her.

ALONE met with a Miss Carter from London to discuss the plight of the older Irish living there. They learned that in the UK, vital services could not be cut off in winter time and in summer, a disconnection must first be notified to the local health authority.

There were reports of vandalism, broken windows, overgrown gardens and a bucket of stones collected in a front room inside the house.

An older man evicted from Grattan Street refused an offer of accommodation in an ALONE house in South Circular Road. He was living in a caravan owned by Sinn Féin which was moved from Ringsend to Grattan Street to accommodate him. Legal aid has been provided.

Another gentleman was moved to the Iveagh Hostel after a spate of vandalism in an area popular with squatters. Many of the buildings had been condemned twenty years ago.

The death and burial of another guest was noted.

Willie Bermingham reported that various items of fuel (including electric fires donated by the ESB), furniture, cookers, etc. were distributed where needed. Outstanding ESB and Gas bills were also looked after together with overdue rent arrears. Electrical work was being carried out on an older woman's home in Crumlin. It was reported that another guest was in hospital and a decision was to be made on whether amputation of his legs would be necessary. The volunteer who did a clean-up of his house found £5,000, which was deposited in the bank for him.

Due to the public outcry at the threatened eviction of older tenants at Upper Grand Canal Street and Leitrim Place by a development company, the matter was withdrawn from the court. Liam O'Cuanaigh mentioned that the ALONE solicitor had been made aware of the organisation's stance on this issue and their support in the future against any such evictions of older tenants residing in some homes for over half a century, with no alternative accommodation.

Liam O'Cuanaigh went on to say how another case of threatened eviction had come to the attention of ALONE before Christmas. In this case, intervention was made on behalf of an older lady living on the North Circular Road to the Irish Permanent Building Society. She had borrowed £3,500 for repairs to the house over twenty years ago but, due to several operations, was unable to meet her repayments. She had incurred a debt over the years of £36,000, made up of the capital and interest together with legal fees. The matter has still not been settled.

SAYING GOODBYE to Willie Bermingham

It's hard to believe that Willie was only around for the first fourteen years of ALONE. Willie died from cancer on 23rd April 1990 but Pat Morgan remembers attending a concert in aid of ALONE in the National Concert Hall shortly before this. 'I still remember it, Willie was in the foyer and the Army Band was playing. He said to me: You'll come to the grand finale?' First of all I thought, Oh God! He's not having another concert! But then I realised what he was talking about. The grand finale he had referred to was his own funeral.'

'Willie Bermingham was in many ways a mystery; people who have known him all their lives still found that he could surprise them. And people who only knew him a few hours believed they had known him all their lives.' The words there of the late Liam O'Cuanaigh,

Newspaper clippings on the death of Willie Bermingham in 1990

paying tribute at the funeral of his old friend and colleague, Willie Bermingham.

Liam began with a wonderful oration on the life and work of Willie Bermingham welcoming everyone to his funeral.

And it was this acceptance and welcoming of everyone, no matter their means or their religious beliefs that brought Willie's funeral to St Patrick's Cathedral, the go-to church for those who had died without family or friends, thanks to Dean Victor Griffen's generosity. Willie's sister, Patricia, recalls that 'Dean Griffin welcomed everyone Willie brought to him, no matter who they were and he really made it very special. That was why Willie chose to have his own funeral there.'

His daughter Kelley recalled Willie's final illness in a tribute to her Dad ten years later.

'The end began in February 1990. Marie – my mother – was in hospital. Nana – Willie's mother, to whom he was so close, was about to turn 79 and Willie wanted to throw a surprise party for her. He was going to postpone it because Marie was in hospital but she insisted that he go ahead. He was afraid that she wouldn't see 80, but little did we know that it was he who wouldn't see his 49th year through. A piper greeted Nana at her gate in the Nurseries, Bluebell, and escorted her just a few hundred yards up the road to our home in Canal Terrace, and thus began one of the typical Bermingham all-nighters! The party went on into the small hours of the morning and, as always, Willie did the clean up before he hit the sack.'

The following morning, Willie asked Kelley to call the lads in the job and ask if there was 'a spare white taxi available.' 'He wouldn't tell me why, and when the fireman in Tara Street asked why he needed one, Willie took the phone from me and sent me up to the kitchen. Needless to say, I went as far as I had to, but I stayed within earshot. I heard him tell his colleague that he couldn't see through his left eye and he'd have to go to hospital. So the 'white taxi' arrived and the lads wanted to wheel him out in a chair, but Willie insisted that he could walk. Being as stubborn as he was, there was no way they could get him to change his mind. His parting words to me were "Don't tell your mother where I'm gone when she rings," and off he went.

We were all brought up knowing the hatred Marie had for lies, and woe betide you if you told her one – she always knew! So when she did ring, she asked how the party went, and I told her the regalia of the night. Then she asked the inevitable unanswerable question "where's Willie"? What could I say? I said he was out – "Where"? And then it all came out. All I could think was, "Janey Mack, Willie's going to kill me for telling on him!".

So, as it went, Willie had to stay in hospital. The suspicion was that he had a detached retina, but that was soon ruled out. Marie insisted on coming out of hospital, even though she was in no fit state, but there were five of us at home – me being the eldest at 17 and David, the 'baby' at 5. Days went by in what seemed an eternity while tests were run.

The bad news came, 'ironically, on Marie and Willie's 18th wedding anniversary – 4th March 1990. Cancer, Melanoma, Inverted. Inoperable. Fatal, 3 months. Our lives had been turned upside down.

'Everyone wanted a piece of Willie to keep and remember, and I recall the flood of people – first to St Vincent's hospital where the staff were caring for him, and then to our home. He never turned anyone away because of the trait he carried – a man who couldn't say 'no' to anyone – even in his hour of need.'

Willie's sister Patricia remembers that even then he refused to leave the phone off the hook, on the basis that someone might need him. She remembers the Wednesday before he died, Spy Wednesday, when a travelling woman came to the door and asked to see Willie. Marie said he was sick and could she be of any help. Willie's bedroom was down the end of the corridor and he shouted out, "Show that woman in to see me". I think she had travelled up from Mayo and her sister was after dying and they had no money to bury her. And it being Holy Week, there were no ceremonies, so he said, "sit down there and give me all your details". So he said there won't be Mass, just prayers and she agreed to that. So he called Fr Bill to come up and they had a plot over in Bluebell – someone had donated another plot there to ALONE. Willie asked her if she'd mind her sister being buried there and she said "no," as long as it was holy ground. So he organised the hearse to drive down to Mayo to collect the body. It was received on Holy Thursday in Bluebell Church and she was buried the following morning, a little over a week before he died himself. He said no-one should ever be turned away from the door.'

Before his death Willie had given away his own grave. This was before the Millennium Plot in Glasnevin and Patricia, recalls 'Willie is buried up in Esker but there are five people buried in there with him. And there was barely any room left when Willie was buried. Another guest of ALONE, a lady called Rose, was to go in after Willie – he had promised her – and Marie kept the promise.' Willie's son, Willie Jnr, himself a fireman, told reporter Conor Feehan in the Evening Herald of 27th April 2015, "Sometimes when a person would die and they would have no relatives the priest would tell dad that they would be buried in a pauper's grave, he had a family plot and he would tell the priest to bury them in it. I think three of them went into his grave before he died himself." Willie died on the 23rd April 1990.

More than 2,000 mourners thronged the streets around St Patrick's Cathedral for Willie's funeral. Carol Flynn in the Irish Press reported that 'the mourners from all walks of life filled the Cathedral and spilled out onto the streets of the Liberties, politicians, Gardaí, union officials, businessmen, Red Cross workers, firemen, musicians and many of the old and poor whom he had rescued from squalor. Dean Victor Griffin told the congregation that Willie had been truly a man of compassion who gave great love and kindness. 'In Willie, the friendless always found a friend, and the helpless always found a helper.'

The President Dr Patrick Hillery, who supported the work of Willie, and his wife Maeve, were among the highest in the land to pay their respects.

Flynn also reported that in accordance with his last wishes, Willie's five children reminded the congregation of his dearest concerns, the lonely, older people, unemployed and destitute. The gifts brought to the altar were a teddy bear, symbolising the united family, vegetables and fruit to remind of the responsibility to feed the hungry, Willie's fireman's helmet and axe, the tools of work representing everyone's right to work, books as symbols of knowledge and enlightenment, and a first aid kit to remind that there are always people in need of help.

In a moving tribute, Rev. William Fitzpatrick, OMI Parish Priest of Bluebell, Inchicore reminded the gathering that a very important person had once come from Nazareth and that Bluebell was a place that was a little bit like that.

Ed O'Loughlin in the Irish Times reported that over 600 firemen from as far away as Cork and Strathclyde formed an honour guard, and the coffin was draped in a Dublin flag, on which was placed a fireman's axe and helmet.

On 29th April, just six days after Willie's death, Aileen O'Meara in the Sunday Business Post explored his fight against rules and red tape in order to help older people. She reported that three weeks before his death he had turned up at a routine quarterly meeting of the Department of the Environment's Task Force on services for older people. 'He was experiencing a temporary remission of his cancer and although walking with the aid of a stick, to the members of the committee he had not changed a bit, despite months of hospitalisation and a knowledge that he was going to die.'

O'Meara quotes Davy Byrne of Dublin Corporation who said: 'He laughed off his illness, he did not want any sympathy for himself, and he just said he would not be around for the next meeting in three months' time.' Mr Byrne went on to describe how Willie had come to him originally 'looking for an emergency gang of people, ready and standing around waiting to be summoned out to an old person's home when one was found. I told him this was impossible, but he went ahead and got Charlie Haughey's support for the establishment of a Task Force and he got a million pounds for it.' Willie and his family and friends were that 'emergency gang of people' but he wanted it to be operated and funded by

ALONE News Bulletin – July/Aug 1984

the State. The late Charlie Haughey had already indicated his interest in the organization and had become one of its Patrons.

O'Meara also spoke to John Doyle, the Eastern Health Board's Manager for Community Care, who said, 'Sometimes he called a spade a spade, and something else as well.' I suppose for someone who came so close to bureaucracy a lot, he might have been a bit impatient. But on a personal basis he was a very easy person to get on with.'

And according to Mark O'Connell of ALONE, Willie 'organized the ecumenical service himself and wrote the inscription for his gravestone. He wanted a service like that because he always liked a big collection of people around him and because he did not want to confine it to just one religion.' And Mr O'Connell added that Willie 'would have been very much aware that there will be a lot of people at his funeral who will be taking credit for the work he has done, people who put obstacles in his way while he was alive.'

On 23rd April 2010, twenty years after Willie's death, Fr Willie Fitzpatrick celebrated his anniversary Mass at the Dublin Fire Brigade Training Centre. There, Dean Victor Griffin paid tribute to his old friend, remembering that 'he would ring me up to arrange the funerals and I would always make sure that the choir or portion of it would be present. Willie saw to it that these unfortunates were at least accorded in death the dignity which they had been denied in life.' And the Dean talked of the mourners twenty years ago who 'bore testimony to one who so freely gave so much of himself to help so many whom the world had passed by on the other side. Willie the Good Samaritan.'

CHAPTER TWO:
THE NINETIES AND NOUGHTIES
- A NEW ERA -
KEEPING THE VISION ALIVE

The nineties and noughties saw ALONE staff and volunteers work to keep what was started in May 1977 by Willie Birmingham alive. Willie may have departed but there was still great need in Dublin to visit and befriend, advocate, house and campaign on behalf of this silent minority. In these two decades ALONE saw its number of homes grow to around 90 units, it continued to advocate on behalf of older individuals and campaign for change with the government and others. By 2010, ALONE had around 90 volunteers befriending older people in the Dublin area.

Following the death of Willie Bermingham, at a Board meeting on 18th June 1990, his widow, Marie, thanked everyone for the expressions of solidarity and work done since his death. She said that Liam O'Cuanaigh had done Trojan work, during and after the period of upheaval, and had helped herself and committee members allay fears of ALONE's guests about their future tenancies. She said she thought it was necessary that a full-time administrator be appointed. Kevin McConville and Pat Morgan were directed to draw up terms and conditions of the Administrator, to be on the basis of remuneration of that of a Dublin Fire Brigade member.

Liam O Cuanaigh – Administrator – (1990 – 1992)
At the next Board Meeting of 11th July, the meeting heard that Liam O'Cuanaigh, who had been very involved with ALONE from the start,

had been appointed to the position of Administrator. Liam held this position for two years, from 1990 to 1992.

HARRY SHEILL – Administrator – (1992 – 2003)

Harry Sheill, the Ship's Captain, took over the running of ALONE from Liam O'Cuanaigh in 1992. But, according to another stalwart, Kevin McConville, they struggled to keep the organisation relevant after Willie died. 'Willie was a very charismatic founder and no-one was going to have the same charisma and nobody did, so it was a big struggle to keep the volunteers interested and encourage them to go on, even though things were looking gloomy. We were no worse than the Franciscans after St Francis died, they had to struggle to get on. We struggled because none of us had the talent to whip up things.' Kevin says they knew they needed the best people possible to keep things going 'and we were very lucky in that we got a very good fellow within a month of Willie's death. Harry Sheill really kept the spirit of the thing alive. He was totally dedicated and enthusiastic. He was another "Willie". I couldn't describe what he has done for ALONE and he still does. He still visits ALONE Walk in his eighties. He is and was a marvellous man.

'Harry's was a holding exercise for a number of years, he was operating on heart and common sense. He was an extrovert and couldn't do enough for anyone, an exceptional person. Harry saved the day and everybody loved him.'

They may have loved him, but Harry was a strong operator to deal with, springing into action when he was unhappy about the treatment of older people. He would fire off letters to those who weren't co-operating and act as an advocate for those no longer able to stand up for themselves. In February 2002, for example, Harry wrote to a landlord on behalf of a woman residing in Rathfarnham to say, 'We are appalled at the threatening letter you sent.' He went on to say that our client, 'a lovely lady, is a widow for the past ten years, she has been very ill and your letter caused her great distress. This type of letter to frail older people living alone finding it difficult to make ends meet is intolerable and unnecessary. We would ask you to respect the elderly in our community and to be more considerate when corresponding with them.'

Harry did not take kindly to politicians looking for unnecessary favours. In October 1994 he received one such letter from a government Minister on behalf of a constituent who 'is very anxious to obtain accommodation in Willie Bermingham Place and perhaps you could consider this matter and let me know the position.' Harry wrote back to say that he had already spoken with the lady in question. 'She is a very nice lady in her early sixties and she already has a nice home. We in ALONE give priority to older people who are homeless and in dire need.'

Harry's letters came from the heart. It was in the best tradition of the type of letter that Willie Bermingham used to send. On 3rd April 1989 Willie wrote to a Reverend Sister in one of the large public hospitals, to say he was 'disgusted and disappointed' with her security staff. He had arrived at the mortuary of the hospital with his family and parked his car. He had a run in with security staff who wanted him to move it. 'His manner was such that I felt most insulted not only for myself and my family and the other four mourners but most of all for the mortal remains of the man.'

Jo McConville, an early volunteer, tells a story which illustrates the lengths Harry would go to fulfil an old woman's last wishes. An old lady had been cremated and she wanted her ashes scattered alongside her dog which had been buried in the Pet Cemetery. 'It was a terribly cold day, the three of us, Harry, Marie Bermingham and myself, had on every coat we had to keep warm. We had the ashes in a shopping bag ready to scatter but the problem was there were a lot of dogs with the same name! I didn't know whether to laugh or cry! We did our best!'

Kevin says Harry's greatest asset was 'that he had a computer in his mind, he remembered everything, also if someone said they needed something, he didn't have to fill in an application or whatever, within a day in a crisis situation, he helped them.' Kevin says, 'often money wasn't the problem, we visited people who had money. The big thing at the time was that the legislation regarding rent control had gone out of fashion and people who owned properties and were receiving fixed rents for decades suddenly found that they would be able to get increased rents. They had big pressure on people who were renting to get out. They wanted to get them out, to refurbish and get big money for it.' He remembers one incident in Dublin's Synge Street, where there was an older gentleman who had paid the same rent since the 1920s. The day he died, entry was forced into his room and the landlord had the locks changed immediately.

PAT LANE – Administrator – (2003-2008)

'I learnt from Harry, "the Master Jedi," he says, 'I doubt if ALONE could have continued only for Harry.' Pat Lane took over the helm on Harry Sheill's retirement. It was the October Bank Holiday in 2003, and he had succeeded in getting a career break from his position in Fingal County Council. The plan was to work for ALONE for one year – but he stayed for five!

The big project at that time was an extension to Willie Bermingham Place in Kilmainham. ALONE was building fourteen new apartments which would bring the ALONE properties up to ninety. The big thing Pat remembers was that joining ALONE was 'like you were coming into a family, that's what it was like. There was no difference between me going home to my mother and father and next door neighbour; they embraced you like that. We had arguments and that but there was that sense that I had become part of a wider family, that was the initial thing. We had a little office in Kilmainham and people would come in and out regularly, they were really coming down to have a

48

chat, they knew you were there to do that and they knew they could trust you. They also came in to pay their donations. There was a sense of friendship, of companionship.'

Pat was particularly proud of the Millennium Plot, which was working very well when he arrived. He recalls a phone call he had from a lady in England to say that her aunt and uncle had both been laid to rest in the Millennium Plot and there was a slight error in the name on the headstone. Her mother was coming to visit the plot and Pat arranged to have just one letter changed. The woman came to visit and was delighted that her family had been cared for so well.

Living conditions for some people were still atrocious in the early 00s. 'Social workers would come to me with problems and you'd go into houses with squalor, rubbish and dirt. You'd have to have a good constitution to go into these places and I'd ask myself: Jesus should I be here at all? But after a while I realised that the smell, the stench, whatever you want to call it, had disappeared. I didn't smell it anymore and why? Because it was the person that I saw in front of me and that was my focus. I'd think: How am I going to help this individual in a way he would like to be helped? Not in the way that I want to help him.

'We'd have a chat, we would suggest clearing out a room and getting a new bed, finding a table and chairs. Would that be okay? But some people wanted to live in the same way. Most agreed the transformation would be a good move. We moved very quickly back then, we'd go straight in with manpower and skips. We were very hands-on! Health and safety considerations might make things very different now!'

Pat has very fond memories of the role that the schools played in fundraising for the organisation. 'The schools were fantastic, you've got to remember that in my era there was no government funding. ALONE was run by donations, end of story.'

Pat says older people are still vulnerable and ALONE is still needed. 'What older people need above everything is social contact. ALONE can provide food and clothing and help with their bills, but the big thing is that social contact; that sense of being a companion with someone, having someone to talk to. If there weren't volunteers, ALONE wouldn't exist.'

The connection with the 'guest' visited by the volunteer continues even when someone passes on and 'we'd all rally round the deceased's family and the volunteer to support them; that was very important. That social contact and the difficulty, when someone passes on, the volunteer feels that. I always treated ALONE as a family, the volunteers, the guests, "no one was alone".'

At the regular induction sessions, Pat would always ask people why they wanted to volunteer. In many cases it was the memories of their grandparents that spurred them on. They'd say 'Things are good, I'm working and I want to give something back.' And that's the type of people we want.

CHAPTER THREE:
THE 2010'S – ALONE TODAY –
'STRENGTH IN UNITY' AND BEYOND –
A CONVERSATION WITH SEÁN MOYNIHAN

This period of ALONE's journey covers from 2008 to the present day under the leadership and vision of Seán Moynihan. When Seán took over, ALONE was still based in the housing complex in Kilmainham, in a small office. The number of volunteers grew to a staggering 600 plus. We saw the introduction of a new role called Support Coordination where ALONE employed case workers to advocate and assist older people navigating around the multiple complex systems that they encounter day in day out in order to get services and changes to their homes. 2014 saw ALONE take on a national role with the establishment of the Befriending Network of Ireland and 2017 saw Netwell Casala in the Northeast of the country merge with ALONE to become one service – ALONE had become a national player in the lives of those isolated and lonely older citizens of Ireland.

Seán Moynihan became CEO of ALONE in December 2008, having spent six years as Director of Services with the Simon Community. He also worked in training and consultancy with a not-for-profit Drugs Task force. Seán recalls his first office in ALONE, which was in the kitchen of a flat they owned in Willie Bermingham Place. 'We ended up with four of us sharing the kitchen and it was so small that I could make the tea beside the desk, I could reach the kettle!' he says.

Seán inherited an organisation where, despite its great work, there existed a 'big hole, a legacy. People weren't sure what to do and different people claimed they were the "keeper of the flame."

In practical terms, this meant that the volunteers and the Trust were very separate institutions. 'The Trust had control of the properties and the money and the volunteers had their own board, their own chairman, their own secretary, everything. They operated separately and independently and the Trust gave them the money they needed. The volunteers didn't trust the organisation!' So Seán took on the role of a go-between. 'I used to run between both of them and I told both sides that the other side thought they were wonderful!' ALONE's first formal Strategic Plan was called 'Strength and Unity' because he wanted to bring the organisation back together. And it worked. The Trustees gave the volunteers positions on the Board, everything was sorted and it was only then that Seán revealed that Strength and Unity is actually the mission statement of Hamas!

'I tried to tease out the image of the typical volunteer but realised quickly that there is no blueprint! ALONE volunteers range from teenagers to nonagenarians, there are men and women from all walks of life, all parts of Ireland and more recently, all nationalities. If there is a common trait, it is the ability to listen and befriend.'

Seán has enormous respect for people who work as volunteers. 'They have deep values and their motivation is really good, so what we had to do was to capture and write down a set of organisational values. We agreed twenty bullet points that encapsulated the values of ALONE and we still go through the list with new volunteers.' Volunteers used to stay an average of six months with the older people but Seán now finds that 'if a volunteer stays a year with us, they usually stay with the older people until the relationship concludes. That will end either by the volunteer moving away or through the older person passing away. Volunteers start off being a social support, and they end up being an emotional support.'

Seán believes that, long term, the key to older people ageing well in the community is community activation, 'so we have over 600 volunteers. We have also undertaken a process to define what volunteer befriending is and should be. We have developed standards and training programmes, supports for volunteers, processes for volunteers to feedback information into the main organisation, we are increasing the number of volunteers befriending an ever ever growing number of older people in Ireland each year. We have also been asked by a number of befriending organisations and groups around the country to set up a network for the over 50 schemes around the country advocating for standards and delivering training to small and large befriending schemes nationally. As well as the services we provide in ALONE, Befriending, Housing and Support Coordination, we provide training, technology, quality standards to all of the organisations. They have no money, and some of them are tiny but what we're doing is trying and keep them going. It means we can help people we never even knew.'

Working for ALONE is not an easy gig. Seán says he knew the week he started that he would have to work around sixty hours a week or leave! Back then there were around fifty volunteers, a receptionist and a bookkeeper and a support person for the guests in the ALONE houses.

There have been huge changes between the ALONE of the late 70's and 80's and today. Seán tried to put it in perspective. 'When Willie started off, the things he was resolving were much more obvious. This was in the seventies and eighties where volunteers were distributing food and bags of coal, that sort of thing, it was very much an altruistic model. The people we work with now have much more complex needs and they're not resolved by one visit or €100. If someone needs €100 this week, they're going to need it again next week, so what resolves that? The needs of older people have changed. Thank God the changes have come because people are living longer, so there are supports needed for people in housing. You can't just give older people a house and think "just give them a house, we don't need to do anything." '

The results of the 2016 Census came out on 7th April. In the period 1979 to 2011 the over 65's population of Ireland grew 200,000 (22 years). However, in the six years from between the 2011 census and

2016 census the over 65s population increased by 100,000 – a staggering acceleration. This acceleration sends many messages, some positive but some not so, it is a warning that the demand for supports and services will steadily grow and grow fast. ALONE is well placed to deal with the challenges coming from a wonderful positive, that people are now living longer. The percentage of older people needing support is probably roughly constant but in reality that means the total figure is accelerating at a rate of knots. Non-profit organisations usually grow at 1%, 2% but because of what's happening, ALONE has to be a solution provider. What's the alternative? 'We could turn around and become hurlers on the ditch and say the government should do what we're doing. It's not going to happen! So you can either take the responsibility, take the accountability on and the chances are if you tell someone else to do it, they're probably not going to do it the way you want it anyway!'

'We must create the solutions. If you take isolation and loneliness, it's an emerging need, it's not just about money. One in ten older people suffer isolation and loneliness to the extent that it shortens their lives.

So what can and does ALONE do?

'ALONE provides: Befriending services, phone services, activities and events, and building a national framework to enable coordinated supports for older people no matter where they are, forging partnerships within the sector, developing understandable models for translation into services on the ground. People might believe that the government should do it, but that model has changed. Government, both central and local, has opened the door for partnership working between the state and NGO sector in many areas of society, so if we're going to take our responsibility and our leadership seriously, then what we've actually got to do is define the problems, be innovative, think outside of the box, develop the solutions, demonstrate the solutions, get the feedback, run pilots, and create models that are scalable and transferable so that everybody across the country gets consistent services, and that's actually what we're doing! We must work in partnership with the government but not lose the right to name what needs to be named.

'Older people can become invisible, people in government have the view that if we give five euro on the pension, then it'll be grand! We're really good at social transfer in this country, moving the money across, but, we're really bad at fixing the problems underneath so in effect what we're doing is masking some of the problems. Older people, especially the ones that we engage with (the isolated and lonely) are afraid to speak out. If you're a recipient of a service, it's really hard to speak out against it. If you're concerned that you might need a service, it's hard to speak out.'

'ALONE wants to keep older people living in their own homes so that they can age at home. Currently you live in your own home and you get a bit of home care or you move into a nursing home. What we want to do is to create, up and down the country, choices around housing. Extra care housing, extra support housing, imagine a house built to universal design, you have your own front door and regardless of whether you get sick or develop a disability or you already have, the building will accommodate you, and the services will rotate around you. It would be cheaper than nursing homes, you might lose 10% – 20% of your autonomy, but you will retain 80% whereas in a nursing home you lose 90%! So, there's a need for choice, and that's what we're working on.

'Each year we have another 20,000 older people added to the population. Roughly 4.6% of our over 65s are in nursing homes. If the only model is to build more nursing homes to meet the changing demographics we would need almost 1,000 nursing home spaces every year. We've needed that for the last ten years and between the government and private developers we are only seeing 500 being made available. Where are those older people currently going? What are their needs? We either need them to be able to remain in their own homes with supports, or we need other choices in their community. What we have to do is try and change the narrative and the story.

'85% of older people own their own homes, and you're always given the view that they should downsize and move on but,' Seán says, 'there are only 30,000 such houses in the country. That's the constant narrative and it's because there are vested interests in moving and selling those houses. Whereas the reality is, if you wanted to downsize, where would you go? What are your choices? Many older people also have mortgages.' Seán says that's going to be enormous over the coming years.

And what of the 15% who never bought a house? Some of them would be among the guests of ALONE, but with rising rents and smaller families, it has become more and more difficult to find a home.

'As I say, ALONE, from its humble origins back in 1977, has been on an amazing and dramatic journey and one that will continue. ALONE will develop more and more homes for older people here in Dublin and, you never know, outside of Dublin. We are planning to develop services around the country and to support other groups and agencies to work progressively to make sure that no older person needs to be left on their own. We are developing strategic relationships with other organisations in the sector, to make sure our campaigning becomes even more effective. We are working with academic institutions to develop technology that will assist older people ageing at home and for help service providers to support older people better and in a joined up fashion. Services need to be there, whatever happens the economy in the next 40 years.

'For ALONE the marathon relay continues, the baton has been handed over many times, from the starting blocks in 1977 to today. The vision is strong, there is unity and direction. Our volunteers are critical to what we do, we are creating a "No Wrong Door" service that many older people need. Most important of all, anything we do places the older person at the centre.'

CHAPTER FOUR:

ALONE
AN ORGANISATION OF
PEOPLE

P eople have always been at the centre of what ALONE has been and is still about today. It is the stories of the older people, volunteers and, more recently, its staff, that is testimony to what this unique and important charity is all about. This chapter records interviews, stories and snippets of who these people are, how they came to be involved with ALONE, and how the organisation has shaped and changed their lives.

ALONE'S VOLUNTEERS
– *SHARING THEIR EXPERIENCE*

From the early days of ALONE, with its small band of volunteer visitors under Willie, to today with over 600 volunteers, ALONE has always and still places high importance on the role that these great people play. Volunteers give up their time to their neighbours who have nobody. The stories below tell of remarkable people befriending other remarkable people. They paint a picture of society, community at its best, looking out and caring for each other.

Why do people volunteer to work with ALONE?

ALONE has a diverse population of volunteers, men and women who set aside time to chat with a stranger. Many of them, however, end up becoming important cogs in the older person's life, an important asset, a regular contact, a friend. If you think about the process in reverse, it's quite something to have a stranger call to your home and, over a cup of tea, identifying a shared interest, to turn *them* into a friend.

I set out to meet some of the volunteers and, of course, they all have their own story, their own reason for getting involved. Many are still involved many years after beginning. A testament to them and to the organisation.

KEVIN AND JO McCONVILLE

Kevin and Jo's (volunteers and Trustee) involvement with ALONE goes back to October 1984. They heard radio reports on people living in dire circumstances, and Willie was very active in it. 'Willie seemed to have a bit of intelligence about him.' He held a meeting every Sunday in Wynn's Hotel, we dropped in and we felt welcome and thought that there might be something we could do, so we went back and volunteered.'

They remember that Willie would arrive in with his briefcase and throw things out on the desk and smoke his way through the meeting. 'He'd take out little slips of paper and read out calls he had got during the previous week. A lot of the time he would have carried out an initial investigation himself and he would read out the details and ask if anyone was near or convenient to the people in distress and people would offer to go.'

'We were all oddballs,' says Kevin, 'the only people who volunteer anymore are oddballs.'

Both Kevin and Jo remember Willie's little bits of advice when he handed out the jobs. 'Very often he would say quietly, "there's a very cross dog there" or "don't go alone," or "he might want some gardening done" which meant the garden was totally overgrown with shrubs and trees and you might be required to do a spot of clearing!'

Volunteering in the eighties involved a lot of visits to destitute older men who lived in the basements of big houses in total squalor in the more affluent areas of Dublin city. They rented their meagre rooms, and Liam O'Cuanaigh, a trustee of ALONE and a photo journalist was the person who recorded the conditions they lived in.

The volunteers tried to look after the most urgent needs of these men, 'If they were hungry or needed to put in an application for home help, we did our best to help them,' says Kevin McConville, 'very often they needed medical help or to get in touch with their families, but most of these men had been adrift for years.'

Many of them were older men who had gone to England for work in the forties and fifties and when they came home they weren't able to look after themselves. At the time the St Vincent de Paul society was also involved in the area. Kevin recalls their role as being very homely. 'You'd get a call from Willie or Marie asking you to go down and see someone and we would report back. It was really down to earth and sensible.'

Willie kept an old store at his home in Bluebell. It was full of blankets and stuff that people had donated to him, there were out of date tins of food and plenty of fuel. Willie gave them anything they needed. There was no talking or planning – if something needed to be done, it was done immediately!

Willie spent Saturday afternoons in his shed. Jo McConville remembers 'he'd have a big fire in the yard and he'd be surrounded by blankets and marmalade and tins and he'd be working on bits of paper. I said several times, "look I could give you a hand if you like"?

' "No, no, I'm fine"! He'd say but towards the end he did say I could help out if I was needed!'

Kevin recalls the sense of shock among the volunteers when Willie died, although he had been wilting fast over the last year. 'Willie himself knew he was going and when he was in hospital, he lay in bed with the door open and called everyone in for a chat. Willie knew but the rest of us were in denial.'

These three worked alongside one another in the ALONE offices. Jo remembers that famous people would sometimes walk in to support them. One person who took a great interest in what they were doing was the Japanese Ambassador. The Japanese have a great commitment to older people and the Ambassador was very interested in what Willie was doing for older people in Ireland. Jo also pays tribute to Willie and Marie's children. 'They were marvellous. When we first joined we'd need something and we'd ring them and they knew immediately what to get us, how to help, they were really great. I always remember the day Willie Junior was accepted into the fire service, he came straight into the office to tell us! He was so proud!'

JEREMY CHAPMAN

Jeremy is a 52 year old mature student. He's studying social work in Trinity College, Dublin. Jeremy joined ALONE 12 years ago when he was a stay at home Dad to his two children, now grown up. 'I was minding the kids and I had a bit of time on my hands. I had also taken a break from acting. My wife heard an ad on the radio and suggested I might like to get involved.'

Jeremy Chapman, an ALONE volunteer, with the lady he befriends, Collette Moore

The idea immediately appealed to him. At that time his grandmother was staying in his parents' house. 'I would have seen a lot of her and we had a good relationship; I always had a lot of time for older people and what they could contribute. So did he see his new friends as surrogate grandparents? 'Yes, and in a good way!'

Jeremy's first match, who he still sees, was a lady called Iris who was living in her own house then, and has since moved to a nursing home. 'We'd go out for a coffee or we'd go to collect her pension, or we'd just go and sit and chat. She is a great character. It was very scary at the start; I think it is for most volunteers. You go in and you meet someone and you're thinking "what if I've nothing to say or we've nothing to say to each other?" Iris is in her nineties now. There was never any fear of the conversation ever drying up! The connection with Iris began when she was in hospital and a social worker suggested linking in with ALONE if she felt a bit isolated and Iris agreed.

'So that's how I was given the call and was visiting her probably for three or four months, and one morning I called and rang the bell and her daughter, whom I'd never met, answered the door and said "who are you"? I said I'm a volunteer from ALONE' "That's who it is," she said, "she's talked about this stranger who calls to visit her and takes her out for cups of coffee and she won't tell me who it is!"

Jeremy says he was a bit embarrassed 'but thankfully I had my identification card. I thought it was quite funny but in a sense it was wonderful because it showed that despite being old she had her independence.'

I wondered about the reaction of families when they learn their relation is being visited by an ALONE volunteer. Jeremy says he has found that families really appreciate it because people live very busy lives. 'With small families, it does spread the load a bit. It's somebody else checking in on your mother or your father to see if they're okay.'

Today Jeremy continues to visit Iris in her nursing home. 'Very often I might be the only person she sees, it's a lovely nursing home full of old iconic pictures that have memories. They make an effort but, at the end of the day it's a nursing home.'

Of course, some people do need the care of a nursing home, but Jeremy feels very strongly that many people are being moved into nursing homes way before they should be because there's not enough home supports. 'If they had more supports at home, they could remain in their own home and that would save the state a lot of money in the long run. It's a no-brainer!'

MICHAEL CLASBY

Originally from Loughrea in Co. Galway, Michael is 77 years old, proving that sometimes the volunteers can be older than the befriendees! Ageism has never been part of the ALONE agenda, and volunteers are welcome at any age. Michael likes the ALONE ethos, which tries to preserve the independence of older people to whatever extent possible.

Michael Clasby, an ALONE volunteer, in the ALONE office in Olympic House

As Michael put it, 'ALONE pursues that very actively with housing and the volunteer system and we're incorporating technology. But the future is a bigger problem as the family model has changed. In the seventies and eighties more family members were living close by and there was a better community spirit where neighbours would check in on one another. But now society has disintegrated to the point where older people are left alone; young people leave home and set out on a path of independence and that came a long way from home. And sometimes, in that process, the old are forgotten or marginalised. Anonymity comes about because of that and they are suddenly alone.'

Michael is very concerned about the dangers of being alone. 'If you believe that nobody really cares, you go in on yourself, your whole mental wellbeing begins to disintegrate, you feel you're not worth anything, that you're useless, you want to pass away, there could be incidents of suicidal ideation, so there's a whole lot of elements including mental health.'

Michael himself is a newcomer to ALONE, having joined just fifteen months ago. He says it was his parents' influence that sent him in that direction. When Sunday Appeal was part of our TV viewing at 6:30 p.m. every Sunday, his parents would always write down the address, and send off a donation. There was a man he knew, Ned, a knight of the road 'and when he passed our house his walking stick would accidentally hit against the door. My mother would know, I'd go out and call Ned in, and he'd have a cup of tea and a sandwich.

My mother never refused a traveller at the door. Those things had a huge impact on me in relation to compassion, the people who were disadvantaged, marginalised, isolated, the forgotten in society, and that has always stayed with me.'

Michael has always worked in the caring services, first as a probation officer, then a Garda welfare officer and then in the adoption services.

Like all volunteers, he will never forget his first visit. Ian was just two years older than Michael (which, he says, gave him a kind of empathy). However, Ian was in bad health and there were difficult elements to the case. He was blind and living in a house which had been rented by his parents since the thirties. He had his room arranged to suit his needs. 'It's a very important part of our training that you take the person as he is, you don't try to change him in any way, you accept his likes and dislikes, you respect his personality, you respect him as an individual and you have a certain amount of compassion. But compassion sometimes can be a useless emotion, you have to do something with it. What I was doing was visiting and trying to fill in parts of his day because he was very lonely. He asked me one day, "do you ever go round your own house and close your eyes and try to empathise with my disability?". I went back and tried it, it was very difficult – I was stumbling over everything.'

Michael and Ian became very friendly. As Michael puts it, 'He was a lovely man with a great interest in films, so we had common ground and enjoyed our chats.' Then, however, Ian was threatened with eviction. Michael explains, 'ALONE and the HSE have been active in trying to help him with this situation but the poor man is finding it very difficult that he has to change accommodation, it is really difficult for him. He is almost 80, and has never lived anywhere else. You can empathise with the worries he has for the future, what it holds for him. Trying to adapt, to new circumstances at his age must be really difficult. It all came to a head when the HSE offered him alternative accommodation but he just couldn't make the decision to move.'

Ian has a great knowledge of Dublin, and great memories of the trams. 'He could direct me to short cuts when I was taking him to hospital once or twice. It was just from memory!'

Michael continues to visit Ian every week. He says he hopes volunteerism is here to stay but is afraid that 'me féinism' could rear its ugly head. 'You don't judge, and you're never adrift, you always have the backup of the organisation. They will tell you what is expected of you. If difficulties arise we can revert to the mentor system or go higher. We will always be listened to, and there is always a resolution.'

ANNETTE GAVIGAN
Just before the Millennium, Annette was working as a volunteer with a Romanian orphanage. She was on the lookout for an Irish based charity to work with and says she knew it would have to be work she would enjoy, so that she could bring something to it. She had always got on well with older people, and she remembered seeing something

years earlier about the work of Willie Bermingham. It stuck in her mind. She met up with the then-chairman, John Maguire. 'He was one of the old-school volunteers,' she says, 'he was a great man and he got me started.'

Annette Gavigan, an ALONE volunteer and Board Member

Annette's first visit was to an older lady, Emer, in Rathmines. 'She lived alone but had a wonderful family network. It wasn't a sad story, her husband had died but she was very mobile and loved getting out and about and her hobby was backing a few horses!' While Emer was always very close to her children, she would tell Annette things she didn't tell them, little worries that she didn't want to burden them with.

Following this, Annette visited another lady in one of the ALONE houses in Kilmainham. We went to Lourdes together – a group of 100 including 25 from ALONE. It was great – we really enjoyed it. But then my little lady fell on a step on the last day and broke her wrist. She made a good recovery, but has since passed away.'

There are lots of things that the new volunteers have to learn as well. Annette remembers her first social in Bulfin Hall in Inchicore. An older man told her he really needed to go home and asked her to order him a taxi, which she did. Luckily enough she mentioned this to another volunteer who took a look at the man's address, and explained that he hadn't lived there for ten years. He was suffering from dementia. As Annette says, 'These are the things you have to look out for.'

Annette, who now serves on the Board of ALONE, believes that there has never been a more exciting time for volunteering. 'We are taking our model which works really well and spreading out into other urban areas around the country, which is really where it's needed.' This includes new projects in Drogheda and Dundalk. 'The befriending has worked so well. We're getting bigger but not too fast, and this is a good thing,' she says.

She still sees the influence of Willie Bermingham in their work. 'He was a radical in his day – his influence is still there. That "getting things done" ethic. The current CEO Seán Moynihan is a very diplomatic man and we need that now. People like Willie are the people we need to start off innovations and initiatives, but generally that type of personality and that type of energy doesn't sustain in the long term and you need diplomacy.'

Apart from the work and the visiting, it's the people you meet in ALONE, really good people, who make it all worthwhile. 'I feel we do the work for selfish reasons. You do it for what you get back and how good it feels. This generation of older people are very grateful and very undemanding and so thankful for the smallest things. A lot of them have so little expectations.' She also believes that as a nation, we don't value old age any more, as in times gone by. 'The older you are the more you know, and I suppose the introduction of technology has taken that away and so older people are not as valued as they used to be. This creates marginalisation. They lived through the Second World War, through huge poverty, recessions, and emigration. It was a different kind of poverty to what we have today, so it's nice to give them some sort of comfort.'

There have been huge changes, even since the late seventies. It's social poverty we're dealing with now – the poverty of company. As the nature of family changes, we're going to have so many more elderly individuals living alone with no family support. We'll have to change to react to that. Also, people today might have drug addiction problems, which wouldn't have been something we had to deal with in the past. Annette feels that 'the last taboo' is elder suicide. 'It's an ugly thought. We hate to think it's possible and it's happening. It needs to be discussed and monitored, so we can grasp the size of the problem.'

SISTER MARY DEMPSEY

Sister Mary Dempsey is a 90 year old nun and is one of the most extraordinary women I have ever met. She starts off by telling me her vivid memories of Willie Bermingham. As Sister Mary puts it, he was 'a great man, he was always there for the people and never thought of himself. He went to the people he was helping. He was no respecter of rank or position – the poor man was as

Sr. Mary, an ALONE volunteer for over 30 years

important to him as the big man.' She remembers that 'Willie gave the Eastern Health Board an awful time because when he'd represent something, and it wasn't done, he'd follow them up. And they'd say "you're interfering in our work" and he'd say "No, I'm not and I'm going to call a press conference – and they didn't want that at all!" He'd say, "unless you do something for this man or this woman I'll call a press conference!" He was very tough to work with.'

Sr. Mary's first visit went on for twenty two years. He was a man who lived in Oliver Bond flats on Bridgefoot Street. Then she turned her attentions to a man living in a flat across the road from the convent in Harcourt Street. 'This man had been in hospital, so I went over one Sunday morning. But he didn't particularly want to see a nun! "What do you want?" he asked me, and I told him I'd been at an ALONE

67

meeting and I had been asked to visit him. "Well you've visited me now, so that's it!" was his retort.'

But Sr. Mary persevered, and went over to him every single week just to see how he was. 'He'd come to the door and say "you've seen me, you've done what they asked you to do and goodbye!"' She asked the advice of ALONE, and they told her to keep up the door stepping.

Then one evening she was greeted with a 'Hello angel' and was invited in for the first time. He was about eighty years old and very poor but the flat was well kept and clean. He was a very well educated man, and had worked in the civil service. The visits continued. One evening Sr. Mary noticed a packet of rat poison on his bed.

'What are you doing with that?'

'Well I'm just trying to get enough courage to take it.'

'So I said, "I'll remove that from you now" and I took it home with me.'

Another time she found a carving knife on his bed.

'What are you doing with that?'

'To see if I have enough courage to cut my throat.'

She took the knife away.

Sr. Mary says they did everything they could to get him to go into a nursing home. However, he refused and eventually he did die, by his own hand. 'He was a lovely gentleman, but very cross sometimes and he'd ask me, "How much visiting have you done? Have you done any training? You're no good at it!"'

Another person Sr. Mary visited had been an IRA man in his youth. He had been interred in the Curragh Camp during the war. He was a fluent Irish speaker and had learned German from the Germans interred with him. 'He had no time for me in the beginning, because I didn't speak Irish to him and he insisted on being addressed as Padraig.

He told me eventually that the great love of his life had become a nun!'

'Sometimes his water would be cut off and he used to come over to the convent. The nuns thought he was lovely! "That lovely gentleman is at the door again!" they'd say.

'When he wasn't well he would call and ask me to call the doctor for him.

'We became very good friends and I got to meet his pals. They were all IRA men. It turned out that Patrick was actually a well-off man and had left his money to an Irish school.

'Sometimes I asked him about his relations, but he didn't want to talk about them. Then one day he showed me a photograph of his brother, who, like himself, had been born in Belfast. He had a niece, so I got the niece's address and got in touch with her. She used to come and stay in the convent and visit him. About two weeks before he died, they had a great chat, she said it was a "valedictory" talk.

It was a very dark October morning when he died. I went over to him to see if he was alright. He wouldn't let me bring over a dinner to him. So I borrowed his umbrella, and he was awful to me when I went back with it. Looking back on it, he was planning his demise. The nurse the next morning called and couldn't get in. I had the keys and we went in and he was dead. But he would only deal with a doctor who spoke Irish, so they got the doctor who pronounced that yes, he had died. He left his body to medical science.'

This old IRA man had a profound effect on Sr. Mary. At one time they suggested he might go into a nursing home, but he said he didn't want to go into any place run by nuns because they'd be worried about his soul. 'I said, "Are you worried about your soul yourself?" "No, I haven't always gone to Mass and that, but I've always prayed," he said. So I told him that the greatest parable Christ ever told was the parable of the prodigal son. I saw him once or twice in Clarendon Street Church. He was a good man in his own way.'

Sr. Mary is always a regular at the party for the blind in Merrion, because one of the volunteers at the beginning, Billy McDonald, used to do it. He died two years ago and they decided to keep it on.

Sr. Mary must be one of Ireland's oldest drivers. 'I'm still driving but I'm not the oldest,' she says, 'I saw a picture in the paper of a man over 100 and he's still driving!'

PAT McCABE

Pat McCabe epitomises the ethic of not trying to impose your own ideals on the people you befriend. He visits two people in Dublin, one of whom is an alcoholic. 'He's a very nice person, and I'm a pioneer, so he'll say to me: "Do you mind if I have a glass?"'

Pat is sixty-eight years old. His involvement with ALONE began when he was working

Pat McCabe, an ALONE volunteer for 14 years

for Irish Rail and they held a monthly collection for charity. When it was Pat's month to collect, he decided to give the money to ALONE. Then, in 2003, he joined up as a volunteer.

Pat is very involved in the annual ALONE holiday, which usually happens in May. They travel around the country and have had holidays in Wexford, Athlone and Carlow. They take about sixty of the older people away. The volunteers arrange everything from the buses to the hotel, the activities, the days out and the nightly entertainment. For many of the older people, this is their annual holiday, and they really look forward to it.

Again, Pat is one of those who believes he gets back more than he gives the organisation. 'I love it, I feel I'm giving back something to the older people.' Pat also met his partner, Veronica, through his work with ALONE. They ended up at the same meeting and he said, "I'll walk you home!"

The rest, as they say, is history.

ALONE – testimonies from its staff today

CORRINE HASSON is a Support Coordinator who began working with ALONE in 2016

'I was initially struck by the passion and drive of every single member of the team, from management to our interns. I knew the job would be tough as you are getting to the core of the problems and issues in people's lives that are causing them much distress and concern, but I knew that the rewards would outweigh this – or so I hoped they would. Within one month of starting, I was able to help an 82 year old man move into one of our ALONE houses. He was at serious risk of becoming homeless and was sick with all of the worry and stress. I will never forget going to the house that day with a card that read "Welcome to your new home" and watching him as his eyes filled up with tears when he opened it. To this day, he still thanks me every time I call to visit, for the support and kindness that ALONE showed him when he needed it most. As he puts it, 'When so many others were closing their doors to me, you handed me a key to my own.'

Christine Hynes is ALONE's Front Office Administrator, who began working with ALONE in 2017

'Every day ALONE receives calls from older people calling in for the first time, making their first step to getting support for themselves or someone they know. Front Office provides front line assistance to those calling from across the nation looking to make that initial connection with ALONE.

'One afternoon in March I received a voicemail from a lady who said that she was alone, living in Dublin and wanted to know if there was someone who could come out and talk to her. A very simple but vital request. When I phoned Bridie back and just told her where I was calling from she began to get upset, she was so happy to speak to someone. She said she didn't drink or go out and over time all those she knew in her estate had died. Bridie mentioned how she had no connection to the new community around her and felt isolated. All she had in this world for company was her dog. When I told her we can look to find a companion to visit her every week it's hard to describe her unbounded gratitude, it made a strong impression on me. She said she felt like she just won the lottery.

'Bridie illustrated how we are all human, how that simple connection of companionship can mean so much to someone who is desperately lonely and how important that first call is to ALONE.'

CAROLINE MULLER began working with ALONE in 2015 and is National Befriending and Support Coordinator

'Working in ALONE gives me the wonderful opportunity to make a direct positive difference in the lives of the older people we support. Nothing feels better than having an older person come back to you and say that the support that we provided has changed their lives for the better. This is what our work is all about and reminds me time and time again why I am doing what I am doing.

'One of the most memorable cases for me was a lady that I assessed for our befriending service. When I went out to see her she told me that it had taken her two years to muster up the courage to refer herself to the befriending service. When I matched her with a volunteer she told me that the visits had made such a significant difference to her and that she felt that she could smile and laugh again. Every time I spoke to her she thanked me for linking her in with our befriending service and that the visits meant the world to her.'

LISA began working with ALONE in 2015 and is Case Manager
'ALONE to me is knowing that we make a difference. No matter how challenging the work can be, seeing first-hand the positive impact that we have in people's lives makes this job incredibly rewarding and I am very proud to be a part of it.'

GARY began working with ALONE in 2013 and is a Support Coordinator
'ALONE is a dynamic and exciting place to work today. The office is always a hive of activity with people working hard to improve the lives of older people we work with. The energy and commitment can really keep you going, knowing everyone is on the same side working towards the same vision.

'Only last year I worked with a lady who had suffered from domestic abuse/elder abuse and social isolation. We linked in many services to deal with these issues and encouraged and facilitated the lady in question to get a voluntary role in a local charity shop. By the time I had finished working with the lady she had told me we had changed her life in a very big way and for the first time in a long time she looked forward to the future.'

FIONA began working with ALONE in 2016, and is Communications Assistant
'ALONE is an organisation I've been passionate about since I initially heard of it years ago. I'm a strong believer in social justice and equality, and for me that's what ALONE is all about. Organisations like ALONE

are so necessary in terms of providing long-term solutions to our rapidly ageing population, and leading the way for others. I was so thrilled to join the team in August 2016 and am excited to continue along the journey, especially as ALONE enters its 40th year.'

MICHAEL began working with ALONE in 2016 and is a Support Coordinator
'In 1978 I met Willie Bermingham, and that had a huge impact on me: he was straight and offered practical solutions to a major need in the community. 30 years later, having worked in the commercial sector, I did a course in UCD and identified what I wanted to do. I joined ALONE as an intern and they offered me a staff position a few months later. I like how they keep that spirit of offering solutions and support.'

MAOILIOSA began working with ALONE in 2015 and is Partnership and Development Officer
'ALONE is on a fast paced journey to make a real difference to the lives of older people. For me it's standing in a room in the Carmelite Centre, Dublin, looking at all the expectant new volunteers awaiting their training and happy to be part of that journey to make that difference. It's the complimentary feedback after the volunteer training sessions. It's the strength of the brand, it's the development of that recognition and most of all it's the volunteers and staff!'

CLAUDIA began working with ALONE in 2016 and is Housing and Innovation Assistant
'Every time I think about what ALONE is up to in Ireland I am moved to tears. After only eight months of working here I have experienced the dedication of the staff, the volunteers and management to make a real difference in empowering older people. I see ALONE as having a massive impact on the quality of life of older people and therefore to society as a whole in the years to come. A future where older people

will experience being a real contribution to society and in turn be honoured for that contribution whether it's in business, communities or relationships. Thanks to ALONE I have had the opportunity to contribute somewhat to that future.'

ALONE – What ALONE means to me: Stories from older people and survey results

AIDEEN ARCHBOLD is a tenant in an ALONE housing unit
Aideen grew up in the Northside of Dublin in the 1940s, one of a large family. Aideen's father was pro-women's rights, believing that 'nothing should stand in their way,' and corralling the boys in the family to do their share of the work around the house. He was also very involved in local community and charity work, with St. Vincent De Paul among others, and was an acquaintance of the late Willie Bermingham, the founder of ALONE. In the late 60s, however, Aideen, keen to travel and a lover of culture, languages and the arts, set off for Rome. Having fluent French, she was looking forward to adding another string to her bow – Italian.

After spending some time with a family in Naples, she moved to Rome. Shortly after her arrival, she met a Jesuit priest who asked her whether she wanted to work part time at Vatican Radio. She did and through this work she met a Liverpudlian missionary priest, a strong advocate of social justice, and, rather unusually for that time, of contraception and reproductive rights. They worked happily together for over 13 years, whenever he was in Rome. When he returned to England, Aideen stayed on in Rome still working as a broadcaster with Vatican Radio.

In 2015 however, after over 40 years of life in Rome, Aideen decided it was time to move home to Ireland. Though she was happy to be back in close proximity to friends and family, she was arriving to a volatile housing market, with skyrocketing rents. After a brief temporary stint renting a room in Artane, she learned that the house was to be sold fairly quickly. She had no other option but to leave. Now effectively homeless, what followed was a frantic search for affordable accommodation, with the help of the Safe Home programme which assists with all the paper work facing older Irish born emigrants wishing to return to Ireland. They had already helped Aideen fill out all necessary questionnaires including signing up to the Social Housing Waiting List. Aideen's place on the list? 200th.

One day, she made a phone call that would save her from falling deeper into homelessness. Prodded by Safe Home, she called ALONE. Within a few days, Keith Lane along with Sue Taylor, current and former ALONE staff members, had organised a meeting with Aideen. She was shown around Willie Bermingham Place, one of ALONE's housing complexes, and completed an interview. After Aideen's second interview, she received a call from Sue. ALONE was offering Aideen a house. Aideen still remembers that day and phone call clearly. 'I couldn't believe it. I was crossing O'Connell Street on a very windy and rainy day and could hardly take in what I was being told. I was in complete shock.' On 19th November 2015, she signed the tenancy agreement. The house was hers, for as long as she wanted it.

'I love Kilmainham, and I'm so grateful for the work of ALONE. They're such helpful, kind and cheerful people who also organise various events for us throughout the year. The work they do is so necessary, and thanks to this organisation, I am very happy to have somewhere in Ireland that I can call home.'

LEO KELLY
Leo Kelly is a recipient of Befriending from an ALONE volunteer
'I find it hard to believe that I am now in my fifth year as a recipient of ALONE's services, or to be more precise the befriending of Eamonn, whom I now consider to be a friend as distinct from a befriending volunteer.

'I have being living on my own since 2000, when my marriage broke down. I was still working in a satisfying job and was occupied and in some ways I quite enjoyed the new found independence. However, I retired in 2005. Losing the social elements of work changed things slowly and imperceptibly. I found I had very few contacts outside work. While married, our social circle was largely directed by my wife. I was happy with that. But that circle evaporated after the breakdown. I spent more and more time just sitting at home not doing much. Gradually I stopped going to theatres, concerts and various events including restaurants. The world seems to cater for couples. Single people are not enthusiastically welcomed in hotels and on touring holidays. So I just gave up. One final note about the road to isolation – the dog I had for 15 years died. That was important, because a dog has to be walked once and sometimes twice a day. Now add smoking, no exercise, staying in and drinking at home, sometimes perhaps too much. Not even going to a pub. I could go weeks on end without anybody calling to the door.

'Eventually I developed emphysema.

'A strong word of praise here for the HSE. The nurse came to see me and suggested contacting ALONE on my behalf. I was matched with Eamonn and we developed what was to become a great friendship over the last nearly five years. Eamonn comes to see me every week for an hour or more. The whole ALONE experience was mainly a confidence rebuilding exercise. Eamonn would go supermarket shopping with me, something I had stopped doing. I have discontinued the meals on wheels service as I now cater for myself. I ceased cigarette smoking about four years ago. The ALONE 4-day holiday every May is a great and joyous annual event. They also organise day outings and dinner dances.

'Over the years it never ceases to amaze me how great the difference these marvellous volunteers make to so many people's lives.'

The voices of older people: Results from 2016 service survey

In a new departure for the organisation, in 2016 ALONE conducted a wide-scale survey to evaluate older people's experiences of the charity's services. The research also served the purpose of gathering general information on service users, such as their age, gender, and quality of life. The study was conducted via a combination of face-to-face interviews and postal surveys, with 84 service users taking part.

Demographics

73% of the respondents were over the age of 70, while the statistics also showed a high concentration of women at the upper end of the age range – eight were aged over 85, in comparison to two men.

In its findings, ALONE determined that the average older person using its services is aged in their late 70s, while there is a broadly even spread of men and women. The older people surveyed by ALONE were largely in good health, with 64% describing their general health as good or okay.

Service users likely to rely on single pension

The survey found it is unlikely for service users to have access to a second pension outside of the State pension, with fewer than one fifth of respondents (16.3%) saying they had a second pension.

The vast majority of respondents, 87.8%, said they were able to keep their homes warm enough. ALONE compared this figure to official CSO statistics, which show 8% of the general population are not warm enough – the exact same level as the survey.

The organisation does point out though that this does not necessarily mean that energy poverty is quite low among older people in Ireland, with various studies – including a Government report entitled 'A Strategy to Combat Energy Poverty 2016-2019' – suggesting over a quarter of the population are energy poor.

Loneliness among older people exists on a spectrum
The survey attempted to get a feel for the loneliness levels felt by older people across the country who are living by themselves. It found nearly one third (31%) of respondents feel lonely sometimes, while 41% have feelings of loneliness either rarely or very often.

ALONE said the results indicate loneliness among older people exists on a spectrum, noting there is little correlation between feelings of loneliness and whether or not a person lives alone or how much time they spend alone in a day. What is concerning from the findings on loneliness is that just a third of older people rarely or never feel lonely.

One of ALONE's main objectives when working with the elderly is to help them feel less lonely, and thankfully well over half of respondents (57.1%) reported feeling less lonely as a result of their interaction with the organisation.

Volunteering – "Older people offer one of the greatest untapped resources"
Being a charitable organisation, it is no surprise that ALONE is always keen to explore new avenues with regard to recruiting eager volunteers and it used the survey to sound out the willingness of service users in this regard.

ALONE said: 'More and more we are realising in the charitable sector that older people offer one of the greatest untapped resources in terms of volunteering.' However, the charity determined that 'unfortunately the majority of respondents stated they would not like to volunteer for ALONE'. According to the study, 63.3% of older people said they would not like to volunteer for the charity, though the organisation notes this may be a reflection of people's general health and age rather than their willingness to volunteer. Just one respondent over the age of 80 expressed an interest in volunteering for the charity. It also found, unsurprisingly, that older people who are in excellent or good health are the most likely to volunteer.

The most popular method of volunteering among those willing to do so was befriending, with fundraising also featuring. Befriending is the primary and most effective and positive type of volunteering within ALONE, as 94.1% of befriending respondents said their volunteer made a difference in their lives. However, what was particularly interesting from the results was the creativity of older people in coming up with suggestions for volunteer activities. Among ideas put forward by respondents were playing guitar, meditation classes, and writing a political news column.

Those surveyed also expressed a desire for befriending volunteers to take them outside the home more, with trips to the dentist and visits to the local supermarket brought up as suggested destinations. Indeed, help with transport needs was the prominent desire among respondents who had visits from befriending volunteers.

The study also helped to highlight the extremely high value of befriending volunteers to older people living alone in Ireland. One respondent said: 'Before I had a volunteer I was completely isolated. She is such a wonderful human being and she has brought such comfort into my life.' Another said their volunteer 'helps me get out and about. He brightens up the day,' while reassurance is crucial for the elderly living alone with one person expressing comfort in knowing 'that it is only a phone call away and they are there for me.'

First impressions last

When asked to describe ALONE staff when first encountering them, over three quarters of older people responding to the study said they were friendly, with further descriptions including 'couldn't be more decent, kind or nicer,' 'more than helpful,' and 'very funny.'

60% of survey respondents rated ALONE's service as excellent, with 80% of older people saying their needs were being met by the service. But service users do not seem as convinced by the charity's check-in calls over the phone. Two thirds of survey respondents said they were 'good,' rather than excellent, while a quarter of housing respondents rated their calls as either 'okay' or 'quite poor.'

ALONE believes this suggests some service users are liable to resent telephone calls in which they are asked seemingly invasive questions, and a personal face-to-face visit may be of more benefit.

Mixed reaction to housing services

The organisation's housing services were also touched on in its survey, with less than convincing feedback from service users in a number of areas. An equal number of respondents found ALONE's maintenance service 'quite poor' or 'very poor' as found it 'good' or 'okay,' although a majority of 55% still deemed the service to be excellent.

There was also a single very negative rating for the housing service overall of 'very poor.' However, ALONE points out 'the slim amount of negative responses in this section may be due to residents' immersion in housing services;' it is easier to be excellent for a single hour a week, as with befriending, than 24/7.'

Strong bond between service users and volunteers

The study found relationships between service users and staff at ALONE remain good, with three quarters of service users rating the check-in calls highly, and most respondents requesting they remain at the same frequency.

Most service users said they felt comfortable discussing any issues or concerns with staff, but only a slight majority said they knew who their support coordinator was. The charity said this shows 'a high comfort level' with support services but 'not a deep amount of consideration of what those services are.'

ALONE also wanted to gauge the interest levels among service users for extra services or community activities. In the main, older people did not seem too keen to explore this avenue; however, responses from those that did showed a distinct interest in being able to access chiropodist services.

The study results hinted at a desire for older people living in isolation to be more involved in their communities. There was a definite curiosity to know one's neighbours evident in the results. According to the responses, 'there is a correlation between not knowing your neighbours and wishing for an introduction to them when they moved in. This suggests that those we identify as socially isolated may wish to be more engaged in a resident community.'

A troubled relationship with technology

Perhaps not surprisingly, ALONE's research found 'a mixed picture of take-up by survey respondents' with regard to the use of technology. While three quarters of service users have a mobile phone, only four out of ten have ever used a computer, and just over three in every ten own a pendant alarm. Those who did have a pendant alarm were predominantly over the age of 85.

Computer usage is more prevalent among older women surveyed by ALONE, when compared with men. Exactly half of female respondents have used a computer, whereas just 30% of men have used one.

ALONE said this 'suggests that women are over 1/3 as likely to use computers as men,' but said research suggested technology and computer use were "based on individual life experience rather than age or socio-economic status.'

Finding out about ALONE

In order to help the charity best reach those most in need of its services, ALONE quizzed older people on how they came into contact with the organisation.

Over a third of older people using ALONE's services found out about it through family and friends, with a fifth doing so via 'another professional,' and slightly fewer finding out through 'word of mouth.' More importantly, 84% of service users who had used the charity said it had made a difference in their lives.

This difference ranged from feeling more confident because they knew a support structure was in place to help them, to giving older people living alone something to look forward to in order to help ease their loneliness. Other survey respondents noted they were happy to be part of the ALONE family, but the underlying theme of responses of older people living alone was the fact they did not feel isolated.

Other responses pointed out how important it was to have someone to talk to on a weekly basis and that 'they are always there when you need them.'

ALONE said the most common emotion expressed towards the organisation in the survey was gratitude.

Lessons learned

The main objective of the survey was to investigate older people's experiences with the ALONE services, and the charity pointed out it was pleased with the 'very positive' feedback.

Some areas of possible improvement highlighted included older people wanting more volunteer hours visiting them. The charity said this first issue 'might prompt ALONE to consider an enhanced befriending service for certain older people.'

On volunteering the study suggested a desire among older people to get involved themselves in supporting others, but the charity took the view that this might not be feasible, given that 'they are often too frail and too old to take part' and concluded it should target 'younger older people in better health' to recruit as volunteers.

Older people using the organisation's services also expressed a desire to do more things with their volunteers, e.g., being driven to the shops.

In response, ALONE said it would aim to recruit more volunteers who drive.

Another common trend among responses was a desire to have more opportunity to socialise with other people apart from volunteers through the befriending service. A third of respondents said they would wish to avail of a space for community activities.

The organisation believes making improvements in this area is very possible and that it could develop a system to identify when residents are lonely and engage with a neighbour's introduction session, for example.

Overall, the results of the survey showed a desire for more socialising and personal contact, which was to be expected.

However, certain specifics were touched on and ALONE has taken a pro-active response to addressing them. This was the first time the charity undertook such a fact-finding mission among its service users. It intends to refine the process and do so again in the future, with hopefully more helpful and relevant issues, trends, and concerns being highlighted that will ultimately help to improve the lives of older people living alone.

CHAPTER FIVE:
ALONE
AND CAMPAIGNING
- CHANGING NEEDS

Campaigning is and has always been at the heart of what ALONE has done. The organisation continues to ensure that what it is learning and experiencing should be fed back to the powers that be. As an organisation it aims to represent the views, experiences and wishes of those who are marginalised within our society.

Since 2010 there has been a swing away from the number of older people dying alone in appalling conditions, but there are new challenges for people who have had the temerity to grow old in Ireland. The work of ALONE has changed somewhat in order to deal with emerging issues. However, it has never stopped campaigning on the issues of the day, just as Willie Bermingham did when he posted those first posters around Dublin or when he successfully ended the practice of pauper's graves or influenced the setup of the Governments, Task Force in 1982, arguably ALONE's first major campaigning success.

Although poverty and loneliness are still at the top of the agenda,

ALONE News Bulletin – Jan/Feb 1988

Ireland's older people have been assailed by a sea of other worries – burglaries or the threat of break-ins, violence and intimidation from drug addicts, even from family members, mortgage problems and the threat of becoming homeless.

Through its own work, and also through its involvement with Government and other organisations looking after the needs of older people, ALONE has had an input into the kind of thinking that both protects and plans for the future of older people.

It has been a watchdog, keeping an eye on government decisions, on cutbacks that might affect older people, and on future planning, which should include specific provision for older people. It has been an innovator, developing new ideas and advocating to make them part of government planning. It has been the national conscience, speaking out when older people are ignored, abused and become invisible.

THE CAMPAIGNS in the last 10 years

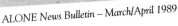

ALONE News Bulletin – March/April 1989

ALONE News Bulletin – March/April 1985

'There when you need us' – 35 year anniversary

ALONE 'Key to Dignity' campaign

ALONE poster – 'Home Alone in Dublin'

ALONE poster – 'Helping Older People in Need'

ALONE Christmas campaign – 'There when you need us'

ALONE poster – 'Most of us enjoy our old age. Some of us need a hand'

ALONE Friendship Week 1998 – 21 year anniversary

Reach Out Campaign

ALONE has always used a brave, unshackled voice to speak up for older people. The organisation has no affiliation and no political allegiance to gag its stance.

2010 was the first year of ALONE's four year strategic plan, 'Strength in Unity.' They distributed €200,000 donated by Bord Gáis to assist older people in crisis with their heating bills, insulated thirty five roofs and began replacing all single glazed windows in ALONE homes, and introduced Core Training. 35% of volunteers completed the four modules in the first two months. They also launched the ALONE Volunteer Handbook, and introduced Garda vetting of all volunteers.

2011 was a tough year nationally, as we coped with the fallout of economic collapse, and the Troika set their sights on Ireland. Chairman Pat Morgan summed up the year for ALONE. 'As services and entitlements were withdrawn, increasing numbers of older people found themselves living in fear and uncertainty about their ability to cope. Through the extraordinary efforts of our staff and volunteers and the generosity of our donors, ALONE faced unprecedented demand. We did not pull back, but by following our plan, we responded to need, and increased our services.'

There were 8,000 requests for assistance via the front desk. Electric Ireland committed to retrofit insulation on thirty ALONE houses, and they ensured security of tenure for their 95 residents through tenancy agreements.

One campaign that received a lot of support in the following year, 2012, was ALONE's response to the announcement of proposed homecare cuts by the HSE. Seán Moynihan called for a reversal of the proposals, saying that older people were becoming more and more marginalised, as a result of ongoing austerity measures. He tackled Minister James Reilly who, he says, 'has repeatedly stated that provision of care in people's own homes is the preferred option. However, these proposals will have exactly the opposite effect, as it will inevitably lead to increased hospital admissions, totally counterproductive if the purpose of these cuts is to save costs.'

2012 was also the year when ALONE marked its 35th Anniversary. A series of events were organised to commemorate the foundation. The ALONE plot in Glasnevin was extensively restored with part-assistance from the Ireland Fund.

The early part of 2013 was marked by allocation of homes to six new residents. A meeting with the Department of Environment secured an extra €1 million funding for the Housing Adaptation grant scheme for older people. ALONE also initiated a project to map befriending services and 130 other services for older people around the country.

In its Annual Report for 2014, ALONE reiterated its Vision Statement of 'a society where older people are included as valued and empowered members of the community.' It pointed out that the organisation's daily work with the people who use their services offers a unique insight into the challenges facing vulnerable older people. 'With over 300 people using our services on a weekly basis, we are acutely aware of the issues they face around poor housing, social isolation, loneliness, health, disability, poverty and elder abuse. In our campaigns, we use the experience of the professionals we are in contact with, and statistics and research to campaign for change and better services for older people.'

The report listed the campaigns for 2014, which included a Pre-Budget Submission to the Department of Social Protection, a submission of two proposals on the Social Housing Strategy to the housing agency, with ALONE one of the few agencies invited to participate in the Housing Summit. ALONE also launched its 'Home Truths' campaign, a national campaign to raise awareness of the number of older people currently in need of housing.

'Home Truths' targeted local election candidates in the run up to the local election. ALONE asked candidates to commit to releasing boarded up properties and unused land to ALONE and other social housing providers so that they could develop social housing. This was very successful, resulting in ALONE securing CAS funding under the 'Special Initiatives for Homelessness in Dublin City' category and Dublin City Council releasing eight units to ALONE for older people in need.

In the 2015 Annual Report, Seán Moynihan focused on our dramatically ageing population. 'The number of over 65s living in Ireland is expected to increase from 606,000 in 2015, to 1.4m by 2046. In ALONE, we believe that in order to meet the challenges that lie ahead we must plan now for effective, high-value, low-cost models of services that will improve the lives of older people for years to come.'

He went on to say that 'the issues we will face in the years ahead are complex, and require equally complex solutions. Working with others in the sector, we are paving the way in defining and solving these problems as they emerge. This is not an easy task, but working together, we can continue to meet the needs of older people as they arise, and make sure the supports are in place to help them age on their own terms at home.'

There were three major campaign in 2015. The first was a question!

'Why are we forcing older people out of their homes?'

Many older people are forced into nursing homes due to a lack of supports to enable them to age at home. HSE figures showed that one in three older people in nursing homes were low to medium care, meaning that they could live at home given the proper supports. The majority of older people prefer to age in their own homes, which makes sense for the community, the economy and the individual.

ALONE ran a national billboard campaign 'Why are we forcing older people out of their homes?' They issued press releases and sent a briefing document on the issues to all Councillors, TDs, Senators and Ministers. Following these efforts, ALONE secured a Private Members debate in the Dáil, held over two nights. ALONE also secured a meeting with Minister for Older People, Kathleen Lynch.

'Homeless in all but name' poster and billboard campaign.
50% of the calls ALONE received in 2014 were from older people looking for support around homelessness or housing. ALONE also saw a huge increase in the number of older people who were being evicted from their private rented accommodation, due to increasing rents. We believe that older people are the hidden homeless. In order to highlight the issue, ALONE ran the 'Homeless in all but name' billboard campaign. This was to highlight the fact that, although we don't see homeless older people on the street, it doesn't mean they are not being left to survive in unsuitable and unsafe housing, or in temporary accommodation. ALONE campaigned for the government to assign a portion of all social housing units to older people, in line with the ageing demographic. ALONE also asked the general public to sign a petition supporting this campaign. They exceeded their target of 1,000 signatures, and sent this petition to An Taoiseach and the Minister for Housing to highlight the issue of housing for our older people.

Nursing Homes Campaign
Should they wish to make a complaint, older people in private nursing homes don't have access to an independent complaints process. 80% of nursing home beds in the country are provided by private nursing homes. ALONE was very concerned that these older people did not have access to an independent complaints process. This means that if they wanted to complain they could only do so to the nursing home itself. This was of serious concern, due to the vulnerability of older people in nursing homes, and the number of disturbing instances of abuse that have been reported. ALONE met with the Ombudsman and HIQA and wrote to all Councillors, TDs, Senators and Ministers, asking them to pass a private member's Bill to give the Ombudsman

remit to investigate private nursing homes. The efforts of ALONE, and those of the Ombudsman, ensured that in June 2015 the law was changed to provide older people in private nursing homes access to an independent complaints process.

#AGE16 Election Campaign
ALONE embarked on an intensive campaign for the 2016 General Election, asking candidates to prioritise the needs and implement plans for our ageing demographic. They were specifically asked to commit to four key aspects, to ensure that Ireland's older population would be supported to age at home with dignity.

These were:

- Greater investment in services in the community.
- Alternative models of housing for older people.
- More secure pensions.
- The appointment of a Minister for our ageing demographic.

Seán Moynihan felt they were very achievable goals for the new government. 'Every year there are an extra 20,000 older people in Ireland, which is expected to grow exponentially. We are just asking that the Government prioritises supports for older people so that we can ensure that Ireland is a place where everyone can age at home, if it is their wish. We urgently need to look at how we can enable a greater number of older people to age in our communities, because continuing with the same model of overcrowding in hospital and emergency departments and high numbers in nursing home care is not sustainable. As well as being what most people want, ageing at home also makes economic sense.'

For the general election, ALONE was part of the #EarnOurVote alliance which also included Active Retirement Ireland, Age Action, Age and Opportunity, Irish Senior Citizens Parliament, Active Ageing Partnership and Third Age Ireland.

CHAPTER SIX:

CONCERNS FOR OLDER PEOPLE – YESTERDAY TO TODAY

For the first twenty years of ALONE the organisation focussed on the grinding poverty and loneliness of elderly people. That hasn't gone away but the new era has brought a fresh set of issues to be tackled. The prevalence of drugs has exacerbated crime against the elderly and intensified the type of crime being committed with murders and robberies destroying the lives of many older people.

In this chapter we look at some of the case studies from ALONE's earlier years and we visit the family courts where, with a large increase in elder abuse, some parents are forced to seek protection from their own children.

Going To Court

A problem facing older people in recent years has been the return of their adult children who are drug addicts. The Family Courts have heard horrific tales of attacks on older people, of having their homes wrecked, their possessions stolen and of older people being accompanied to the post office to have their pensions stolen by their own children.

There is also the hidden problem of gangs tormenting older people when a son or daughter runs up a drugs debt. These are the problems that didn't exist or were minimal in the time of Willie Bermingham, but they are issues which scream out for ALONE to continue to tackle the problems facing older people today.

Older people come to court seeking barring or protection orders against their adult children but they often just stand there and sob at the enormity of what they are being forced to do. Some of them come to court with injuries and bruising and, although reluctant to ask for the Orders, realise this is necessary.

Below are some examples of the traumatic cases faced by older people in court. They are taken from 'The Family Courts,' published by Blackwater Press.

One woman who came to Dolphin House (the specialist family court in Dublin) sought a barring order against her adult son who lived with her. He didn't contribute anything towards his keep, abused alcohol and drugs, verbally abused her, swore at her and had threatened to kill her. She said the Gardaí and the social worker had advised her to go to court. She was granted an interim barring order. In these cases the full hearing is set for another day when the other party, in this case the son, is given the opportunity to come to court to explain why the order should not be made permanent.

In another case, an older women, the mother of a drug addict, came to court seeking a safety order against her son. She said he was making her life 'hell.' He owed money to people who came around to her house demanding it from her. They threatened her because she couldn't pay her son's drug debts. The son called her names and had smashed two television sets.

Gardaí had been called the previous day and when they arrived, the house was full of smoke. She thought he had tried to set fire to her home. There were other members of the family living in the house and she said they were particularly frightened when he held a knife to his sister's throat. Gardaí had advised her to get the protection order. The sister who had had the knife held to her throat also gave evidence and said she was petrified.

The judge told the mother, 'I have a reasonable fear for your safety,' setting a date for a full hearing when she said she may issue a safety order.

Gardaí were called five times in one day to the home of another older woman, whose son went on the rampage. He was on drugs and he kicked in the hall door, smashed up the house and caused terrible damage. His mother was in court seeking a barring order. She said she was very frightened and wanted her son to leave the house for good. When she told the judge that she didn't know if he was in the house at present, he told her to get a garda to escort her home and granted the interim barring order.

Another older woman turned up for a full hearing of her barring order application against her adult son. There was no appearance by the son, but the court heard the full details of the case. The son was taking cannabis and cocaine. He had attacked his brother in the family home. There was blood all over the hall and the walls but he wouldn't stop the attack. He grabbed his mother's handbag and then went on his knees and threatened to kill himself. The Gardaí were called and removed him from the house. 'I can't live like this anymore,' she said.

An older man was up next, seeking a protection order against his adult daughter who lived at home. He said the daughter drank a lot and there had been an incident where she had slapped him across the face three times and then climbed out the window. His wife was afraid to be alone with her. The judge granted the father a protection order.

'There will be blood spilt here today if I don't get my money!' That threat, from a man in his forties, was the reason his father came to court seeking a protection order against his son. He said his son had broken up furniture and came upstairs with one hand behind his back. 'He has a knife,' warned another family member. Judge Gerard Furlong pointed out that he could, as a parent, consider seeking a barring application. The man, however, said no, he would try a protection order first and a temporary safety order was granted.

Finance

Money has always been an issue for many older people. Some would assume that they have reached a stage in their lives where they are comfortably off, the mortgage paid, the pension coming in weekly. For many older people, this isn't the reality. A growing percentage of older people still have a mortgage to pay, and often from a reduced income. Many, especially women, are not receiving the full rate of social welfare payments because they took years off paid employment to rear their children. Others have come home after a long life spent abroad and are renting. It is the older people in the rented sector who are most vulnerable, living at the whim of landlords and concerned about their future. ALONE is still battling landlords and evictions, as it did forty years ago.

Marriage breakdown is also a factor in having little money. The cost of keeping two households going can be very debilitating. The fact that people marry at an older age now also means that they could still have dependents late in life.

So, where does the scrimping start? Food and fuel are the first cutbacks for older people not looking after themselves properly. There are many incidents of older people being admitted to hospital suffering from malnutrition and cutting back on food in order to pay the bills. There are countless reports of older people trying to get through the winter spending as little as possible on fuel.

Some older people do ask for help, but the need is not always apparent. This is why ALONE's policy of keeping an eye on a neighbour or of including someone in their regular visits can make a huge difference.

Regarding mortgage arrears, the Phoenix Project, which assists those in trouble with banks and building societies, has seen an increase in older people being forced to give up their homes following trouble with mortgages. In many cases, the organisation has been able to assist them by rescheduling their borrowings. CEO William Prior lists cases of older people living in cold houses, afraid to turn on the heating, of a couple in their seventies who lost their home and their business, who were still being pursued by the bank for the money that it claimed they still owed.

Crime

Crime is one of the biggest concerns for older people today, with a long list of older people who have been broken into, terrorised, attacked, murdered and robbed, sometimes for a tiny sum of money. Thieves have destroyed the peace of hundreds of older people, some of whom never get over the trauma.

It's not just in Dublin that older people are targeted. In my work as a journalist, I have reported on many cases around the country. One of the worst was an attack on two sisters, 89 year old Suzie Arthur and her sister, Isa (91), who lived independently near Raphoe, Co Donegal. In the middle of the afternoon, three men entered their home, the house where they had been born and lived all their lives. The men had called to the house a couple of hours earlier offering to paint the house. They left when Isa told them 'no,' but then returned. Suzie broke her hip when they threw her to the ground, and she died on October 11th 2013. Isa left the house for some time, but then decided that the raiders were not going to get the better of her. She returned home, but died on 17th March 2015. At the inquest, the coroner said the burglary had resulted in the deaths of two people. 'We have two ladies whose lives were totally turned upside down by one incident,' he said. 'This is a terrible tragedy and I think it is a disgrace what happened.'

Joe McClean, the women's nephew, told the Donegal Daily that the two sisters were not married and had lived at the house all their lives. "The garden was their pride and joy. It was their thing in life," he said.

"The incident resulted in the death of two people, and that is a terrible thing. It was callous, cruel, unlawful and it was wrong," he said.

Another attack on an 89 year old woman occurred in Bray, Co Wicklow, when Eva Sutton was beaten up by two men who ransacked her home. She was left with broken ribs, a broken nose and many other injuries.

Her quiet, peaceful life was destroyed by these men and she has not been able to return to her home. In April 2017, her attacker, a 23 year old local man, was sentenced to ten years in prison with the last two suspended.

And ALONE records tell of a 76 year old woman in Galway who had both her arms broken by an attacker who stole her handbag as she walked to the local shop. In another incident, two sisters aged 84 and 87 were punched by three men who tied them up in their Co. Kildare home, before stealing some cash and valuables. There was another story of an 80 year old shop keeper and his wife who were terrorised by a gang who burst into their house as they watched television. They were tied up and beaten as their home was ransacked.

This lack of respect for older people is not a new phenomenon. As far back as December 1993, the ALONE newsletter said 'your local friendly thug is going for the easy target – the elderly living alone.' It said that volunteers increasingly have to bring up the matter of security (without alarming the old person if possible), and after an initial friendly banter, things like locks on doors, catches on windows, emergency lights, personal alarms and telephone hotlines have to be discussed.

At that time, 24 years ago, it said a drug addict needed at least £100 a day to feed the habit. 'But it's not just addicts who are terrorising society,' it said, 'there is a shady world of theft, laundering of stolen goods and violence, barely suppressed, and if society does not deal with it, and the injustices which bring it about, then society as we know it is doomed.'

It shows a photo of an 83 year old man, Denis Kirwan, whose Terenure home was broken into. He was grabbed by the throat, and his life savings of £135 were taken. There was a happy sequel, however, when an anonymous well-wisher called to the ALONE office some weeks later with a gift of £135 to replace the stolen savings.

Even 28 years ago, in 1989, the late Irish Times journalist Mary Cummins described in An Irishwoman's Diary how she sat with an older couple whose home was under siege from local children who were tormenting them by throwing stones, empty cider bottles, iron bars and even a bedstead at their home. 'One hot and sunny afternoon I sat with them in their darkened sitting room. The gloom was caused by the heavy wire netting that protects all the back windows. They do not whinge or moan; but a sense of hopeless frustration pervades their voices. They are almost completely housebound and see few outsiders.' But then Mary spoke to Willie Bermingham and 'his instant comprehension of what was involved combined with an impression he imparted that there were ways of solving many problems threw the first chink of light on what had seemed a long, dark tunnel.'

In the early nineties, ALONE supported Dublin Corporation, the Eastern Health Board, the Department of Health, the Gardaí, and a number of other voluntary statutory bodies including Vincent de Paul, Victim Support and Age and Opportunity in launching the 'Reach Out – Be a Good Neighbour' campaign. At the launch in 1994, Michael Kelly, the chief welfare officer with Dublin Corporation, said that older people living alone felt particularly vulnerable and some became prisoners within their homes.

Sadly, these are not isolated incidents. A quick look through most newspapers will tell similar stories. ALONE has been very active in asking people to keep an eye on their older neighbours. Neighbours play a vital role in the protection of older people. Visits can discourage would-be raiders who might be casing an older person's house. The people to watch out for include door-to-door salesmen, as well as anyone hanging around and looking suspicious.

Another danger to older people comes from callers trying to intimidate them into having a path tarmacked or to have 'repair' work done on a roof. The airways are flooded with calls where people have been duped and threatened into going to the local ATM, accompanied by the caller, while they withdraw their savings to pay for something they didn't need in the first place.

ALONE – Influencing the future for older people

In order to plan for the future needs of older people in Ireland, ALONE has, over a number of years, published professionally researched position papers on various aspects of successful ageing. These are crucial to government and NGOs in terms of forward planning assistance, lateral thinking and public spending. They cover Housing, Health, Loneliness and Services and Entitlements and are regularly updated.

Core to these papers is the fact that we have a dramatically ageing population. By 2026 16% of the population will be over 65. Each year, the population of over 65s increases by 20,000, and will do until 2040 when it is estimated that there will be more than 1.4 million people living in Ireland over the age of 65.

Ageing at Home

Providing housing for older people has always been at the top of ALONE's agenda. The organisation has now provided two small housing complexes that it continues to run successfully as well as 53 ALONE houses scattered around the city, which ALONE's most vulnerable older people can now call home.

Supporting older people to age at home makes sense to the individual, to the community and the economy. There was an additional €10m in new development funding announced for homecare in the last budget. However, despite an overall increase of €82m in older people's services, over 50% of older people awaiting, or sent to long-term care (nursing homes) from hospital wished to remain at home, and could have done so. ALONE also points out that it costs three times more for nursing home care than home help and up to 15% of people are not involved in decision making, with this figure jumping to 45% for those diagnosed with dementia.

These figures tell us a lot about our concern as a people for the autonomy of the older person. It really is only when we see the actual figures that we realise how our older population has been pigeon-holed into economic or disease-led categories, where their own preferences for care are being ignored. Perhaps it's just too easy to ignore them, because the alternative, although cheaper, involves a spot of lateral thinking, of finding ways to keep an older person at home, when the nursing home seems like an easier option.

So, as of 2013, why does Ireland have one third more older people in nursing home care than the EU average? ALONE points out that Ireland has a very underdeveloped care model for older people, compared to some of its European counterparts. Ireland is ranked 15th in the Global Rankings Index in terms of countries' care for their older people.

ALONE has conducted a cost comparison on the various options for caring for older people. At time of print:

- The cost of an acute hospital bed is between €800 and €900 per day.
- The cost of a nursing home bed per day is €100 and €200 while Nursing Homes Ireland puts the average cost of a bed per day at €128, but that can vary greatly between the most expensive Dublin (€157) and least Donegal (€107).
- The cost of home help three times a day is between €50 and €70, according to the Irish Private Home Care Association (IPHCA). The average cost per hour of home care is €17.61 (€52.83 for three hours).
- The cost of ALONE housing with supports is €34 a day.

ALONE is adamant that there is not enough support for Home Care Services, pointing out that almost 90% of home care is provided by unpaid family carers, at an estimated cost of €4 billion annually. It also criticises the practice of 'care cramming,' or the provision of very short (e.g. 30 minutes) care packages as inefficient, preventing meaningful service from being delivered.

ALONE says we are forcing older people out of their homes and their communities through a lack of finance for home help hours, home care packages, mobility aid cuts and a lack of supportive housing.

Home and Community Care Ireland has stated that some 34% of patients in long-term nursing care with low to medium dependency would be more appropriately cared for under enhanced home care packages, with potential annual saving of some €69m from 2014. IASW and Age Action's recent report says that half of all those awaiting or already sent to nursing homes from hospitals could be cared for in their communities.

At the end of life, according to the Irish Hospice Foundation, one in four deaths that occurred in acute hospitals could have taken place at home, if the necessary supports were in place.

Elder Abuse

There are a number of risk factors for elder abuse. Those over 80 years of age, women in poor health and with a low income, those with mobility issues, a cognitive impairment, dealing with depression, and a poor social network are most at risk.

Older people with three or four of these risk factors are nearly four times more likely to experience abuse, while those with at least five of these risk factors are 26 times more likely to experience it.

ALONE represents the one in five people who are homeless, socially isolated, and living in deprivation.

The organisation wants to see more effective monitoring of residential care homes in order to prevent future elder abuse. It is also calling for enhanced regulation in the care sector to increase the protection of vulnerable older people living in residential care and the community.

A 2010 study by the HSE of more than 2,000 older people living in the community showed just over two in every hundred 'older people' had experienced mistreatment in the previous year.

Going by 2007 census figures, this would put that number of older people experiencing mistreatment at 10,201.

ALONE takes its lead from the World Health Organization, which characterises elder abuse as 'a single or repeated act or lack of appropriate action occurring within any relationship where there is an expectation of trust, which causes harm or distress to an older person.'

It encompasses physical, psychological, sexual, and financial abuse, as well as neglect and discrimination.

The HSE study cited by ALONE in its position paper on elder abuse indicates financial abuse to be the most frequent type reported, with women more likely to fall victim.

It also suggests people over the age of 70 are twice as likely to face mistreatment as people in the 65-69 age bracket.

The highest level of mistreatment was found in older people who were divorced or separated, and those living in intergenerational households.

Sadly, the HSE research also determined that adult children are the most likely perpetrators of elder abuse, with half of incidents reported falling into this category.

Between 2008 and 2014, more than 15,000 cases of elder abuse were referred to the HSE, with the numbers worryingly rising each year within that time span.

In its position paper on the issue, ALONE points to a 2013 study of older people in Ireland that found many older people, though concerned about specific physical and psychological vulnerabilities, saw oppression and ageism as the most recognisable form of elder abuse.

It therefore argues that responses to elder abuse should value the independence and autonomy of the older person involved in an abuse claim.

The study itself suggests these values should be advocated for at a societal level.

The charity also believes that regulating home helps would lead to a safer environment for older people still able to live in their own homes, while it also advocates increased investigative powers for HIQA to enable individual complaints to be explored.

For example, at present, the complaints procedure in nursing homes requires older people or their families to lodge a complaint within the home itself, i.e., directly to the perpetrators of the alleged abuse.

The nursing home then addresses the complaint and registers the complaint with HIQA.

Only where the complainant is unsatisfied with outcomes can the Ombudsman investigate.

HIQA does not investigate individual complaints – just the nursing home's handling of that complaint.

ALONE points out that 'clearly, this is not a satisfactory procedure.'

Central to the organisation's proposals for the management of elder abuse is to empower older people to manage the situation themselves.

It believes the development of partnerships between specialising in the care of older people would bring about 'innovative strategies to empower older people to report cases of elder abuse.'

The charity is adamant that 'an empowerment model needs to be established to rectify this.'

It also suggests that story sharing in a peer group setting could help raise awareness of elder abuse boundaries and lead to a tolerance for such behaviour to be questioned.

CHAPTER SEVEN:
ALONE HOUSING

The provision of decent affordable housing for older people was one of the first aims of ALONE forty years ago. The organisation started to buy small city centre homes as funds permitted, where today ALONE's guests continue to live.

However, Willie Bermingham and the organisation had bigger plans and in 1986 opened a ten unit complex to be known as ALONE Walk in Dublin's Artane.

'Níl aon tintean mar do thintean féin' reads the inscription on the stone at the entrance to ALONE Walk. The sod had been turned by 92 year old Michael Dunne, the oldest person visited by the volunteers and a man who knew WB Yeats, Countess Markiewicz and Seán O'Casey. Michael's home had been without water, a working toilet and adequate roofing until the Task Force moved in. Journalist Mary Maher described the celebrations for the turning of the sod ceremony in the Irish Times on October 8th 1984. Complete with the Artane Boys Band, 'It was very much a neighbourhood party,' she wrote, 'with children, dogs and teenagers, and everyone invited for a cup of tea in the nearby garage.'

The ceremony coincided with the opening of Active Age Week, 'a promotion to increase community awareness of the needs of the elderly' being jointly undertaken by Dublin Corporation and the Eastern Health Board. 'But,' wrote Maher, 'Mr Bermingham and ALONE maintain a polite but distinct distance from official activities, and see themselves as an independent pressure group seeking Government action rather than a collaborating charity. "We are just continuing to do what we have been doing and there's no wiffle-waffle about it," he said.'

Then on 1st June 1986, building finished and Padraig Yeates reported in the Irish Times that over 200 people had attended the opening of Ireland's first custom-built and privately-owned old people's complex in Artane. 'The developer of the €300,000 project, which has ten dwellings, was not a speculative builder, however, but the ALONE organisation.'

Sick man found in squalor

By Donogh Diamond

Neighbours and relatives of elderly people have been urged to check constantly on them after a 67-year-old man was found semi-conscious in his derelict south Dublin home.

Gardaí broke down his door after being called in by a worried neighbour on the south quays. They found rats on the floor of the same room.

The elderly man was collapsed on a pile of rags which served as a makeshift bed on the lower floor of the two-storey house. Damage to the roof of the house had made the upper floor totally uninhabitable and the house was without electricity, water, cooker or toilet, said the old people's voluntary organisation, ALONE.

The man was taken to hospital and medical staff are now deciding whether he would be capable of fending for himself if his home was totally refurbished.

ALONE administrator, Mr Liam O'Cuanaigh, said that the organisation came upon cases like this "every other winter." "Severe weather doubles all the problems of elderly people living alone," he said.

He cautioned people not to fall into the "rent-a-granny" Christmas trap when old people were fussed over at Christmastime only to be left alone for the other 51 weeks of the year.

Evening Herald, Saturday, April 20, 1991 3

Proud day for family as Bermingham Place is opened

WORK IN PROGRESS ... Alone administrator, Liam O Cuanaigh, with Alone trustee, Pat Morgan, at Willie Bermingham Place

COMFORTABLE ... the interior of one of the houses at Willie Bermingham Place

A dream comes true for Willie

By PAULA McMAHON

DUBLIN fireman and founder of Alone, Willie Bermingham, holds a very special place in Irish people's hearts. Now a housing complex called Willie Bermingham Place means there will always be a special part of Dublin dedicated to his memory.

Official opening of Willie Bermingham Place in 1991 with the Lord Mayor

By WILLIE BERMINGHAM

A FEW years ago, on New Year's morning, an old woman was found dead in her bleak little flat on the south side of Dublin. On the table lay an unopened Christmas hamper.

On the same morning, over on the North Circular Road, a 75-year-old who had had five operations for stomach cancer was found frozen to death on the floor of her basement kitchen. Her flat, too, had some external trappings of a "happy" Christmas.

woman who   Summerhill area

A sad piece of news from the Irish Press from December 24, 1984.

Not very cheerful thoughts as the fairy lights blaze and people carry home twice their weight in food and drink. But as one journalist remarked after he heard these stories: "It keeps you from sulking just because the turkey tastes tough."

Do the neglected old know it's Christmas time at all? Of course, they do. But they know as well the great desert of loneliness that follows — all 51 weeks — until the carol singers and the hamper deliverers emerge again.

It's that gnawing loneliness that eventually leads many overlooked old to despair and self neglect. Something falls in the kitchen. They don't pick it up. A toilet freezes up. They don't bother to call for help. The nights are cold. They stay in bed with a few clothes thrown on top of the blankets. The roof starts to leak. They just move their few possessions to another part of the room.

Christmas time brings a lot of welcome, if meaningless, fuss. Reactions appear for a few minutes and promise to call again fairly soon. They rarely do.

Cards come in from old friends and workmates, but are never followed up by a handshake and a cup of tea beside the fire. Food hampers are delivered from many sources — some containing goods that couldn't be digested by a hungry athlete.

Some of the old timers will be on someone's party list. While the majority of them are delighted to go to the old folks' parties, not a few are dropped off at a steet corner when it's over to spend the night in a cold and barren room which nobody bothers to enter.

It's not that people don't care. They do—but they often don't think. If you were lonely and cold and living in fear of muggers and vandals ,not to mention being harassed by a landlord, would you rather have a fiver or a good friend?

At this time of year, our volunteers in ALONE step a little into the shadows. They may feel they are intruding on a "family" holiday, or even feel embarrassed at finally meeting the relation the old old timer has talked about—but hasn't seen—for the previous twelve months.

The volunteers are asked, however, to get back into circulation immediately after Christmas ,before the dark depression of the New Year begins to claw away at the old person's confidence.

There are probably no official statistics, but undertakers have told us that they bury an awful lot of old folk before spring time. How many of them, I wonder, die from old fashioned broken hearts?

I have been asked for a few "tips" on keeping old people safe this Christmas. Contrary to some notions, ALONE doesn't own the old people of Dublin no more than the Health Board owns the sick ones or the Simon Community the homeless ones. What you can do for the old folk depends on the old person's needs when ASKED · about them and on the level of interest of the neighbour or visitor.

But there are a few obvious steps. Hypothermia or freezing to death is a great risk where an old timer has insufficient bedding or is not getting exercise and nourishing food. If an old person is found in extreme cold, don't attempt flash heating, but warm the

Images of poor housing conditions ALONE has come across in their work in recent times

Willie Bermingham Place site – Dublin in 1978

Opening of ALONE Walk – 1986

Yeates went on to describe the features which made the flats special for older people, features such as 'rounded corners, special light switches, toilet locks that can be opened in emergencies and ramps and smoke alarms to make each unit not only comfortable, but safe for the new tenants.'

The other very special feature was that each unit was named after an older victim of homelessness in Dublin. 'Number 4, for example, is named after Mary Miller, who was found dead at the age of 87 in a rented home on the North Strand, where the slates had been removed from the roof, the outside toilet bulldozed and the water and electricity cut off. Number 7 is Anthony Burns House, named after a Co. Tyrone man who had moved south to escape the Troubles in the 1970s. Anthony was a victim of the Supreme Court decision that led to the decontrolling of 30,000 rented dwellings four years earlier. When his landlady decided to evict him, ALONE took up his case in the courts. However, the strain was too much for Anthony, and he was found floating in the Liffey three days later.

Mary Limebear House is Number 9 and marks her death and that of her 50 year old disabled son, John. At 74 Mary had had six operations and could barely look after herself, let alone John, who was confined to his cot. She had placed jagged shards of glass around the skirting of their basement home to keep out the rats and often sat up through the night with a kitchen knife to drive them off. Hypothermia killed her on New Year's Day, 1978. John died a year later in the same condition.

Dolly McDowell was a 1916 veteran and Number 11 is named after her. The 90 year old was trapped by serious illness in a two-seater couch where she lay undernourished, dehydrated and with ulcerated legs for over a month.

Fast forward to 15th April 1990 when Willie Bermingham took the shovel and turned the sod for ALONE's second residential complex at Kilmainham Lane. Watching him were his wife Marie and his children Anne-Marie, Kelley, William, Seán Paul and young David Francis. This was to be Willie's last public appearance before his death – eight days later on 23rd April.

The new apartments, which cost €2.2 million, were funded by the Department of the Environment, Dublin City Council and from donations to ALONE. The half-acre site was just a disused patch when ALONE acquired it in 1989.

Residents were required to sign an agreement which stated that they were considered to be permanent guests of ALONE. They were not levied with a rent, though they could make a contribution to insurance and maintenance costs. 'For guidelines only, it is suggested that residents contribute around ten per cent of disposable income.'

There were no serious restrictions for the residents. They were reminded that this was not sheltered accommodation and they had to make their own arrangements regarding medical care, electricity, cable TV, etc. It was their home and they were welcome to have a pet or to have friends stay over. There is a garden in Willie Bermingham Place in which residents and volunteers have all taken a keen interest, which has taken 1st prize Senior Citizens Complex and 1st prize in the Dublin City Council Neighbourhoods Awards in 2015.

Today ALONE has 100 housing units across Dublin, and plans to develop more over the coming year.

CHAPTER EIGHT:
ALONE: THE GOOD TIMES

One of the great successes of ALONE has been in bringing companionship and happiness to so many older people around the country. Willie Bermingham asked that no-one would be left alone and in the 27 years since Willie's death, the organization has lived up to that ethos.

Last Christmas a wonderful thing happened. The people ALONE visits turned the tables by inviting their volunteers to the cinema. But there was a secret! When the cameras rolled, they saw that the elderly men and women had got together to make their own short film thanking the ALONE volunteers for being part of their lives.

This is what they said...

'When eventually I retired from my employment, I had been working about 40 years, and I came home here, it was on my own...'

'I wish that I had a family...'

'We laugh a lot you know, we laugh and talk all the time...'

'Thank you Margaret for being so kind and so patient and I know you must always have a terrible headache when you leave me...'

'Colette...you're the most wonderful thing that has happened...'

'I have not got any word to tell Mary thank you, it's not "in the dictionary because she means too much to me...'

'The minute she walked in I knew we were going to be good friends and I feel I have known her all my life...'

'Thanks Pauline for being a good friend, you've been a good friend...'

'Aaron, you're on candid camera, thanks very much for everything.'

'Eamonn to me is priceless…'

'Thank you doesn't even cover it…'

'I would like to say thank you.'

As the film was shown, the speechless volunteers, who were sitting beside the friends they visit, were showered in flowers and smiles. There were some tears and a great deal of happiness.

Photos of ALONE events

Tony McCarthy and Noel Murphy at the 2017 Larkin Community College St. Patrick's Day Lunch

Annette Egan and students from Larkin Community College at their 2017 St. Patrick's Day Lunch

ALONE 2017 Walk
Volunteer Day with
Doosan

ALONE Christmas
Campaign 2016
– Anne Doyle,
Brendan Crean,
Eithne McGrane

ALONE Christmas
Campaign 2016
– Brendan Crean,
Eithne McGrane,
Seán Moynihan

ALONE *Spring Dinner Dance 2017*

ALONE *Summer Holiday*

CHAPTER NINE:
... AND A NEW BEGINNING.

On Tuesday, 23rd May ALONE celebrated 40 years of its work by volunteers and people involved with ALONE over the decades. There was a buzz about Dublin City Hall from early afternoon as ALONE staff set up photo displays and banks of memories from the first 40 years. Then the crowds began to arrive, smiling, laughing, hugging, delighted to be part of this auspicious occasion. There were guests sharing stories from their ALONE holiday and warning me 'Don't dare put that in the book!' Then we all settled down as Pat Doherty, Head of Strategic Development, Housing and Funding, took to the stage and, to delighted applause, told the audience 'This is a big night for us!' The big stone clock over our heads showed that we had started an enthusiastic four minutes early! A huge celebration cake with the '40 years' logo sat in front of the stage.

The Lord Mayor of Dublin, Brendan Carr, then addressed the audience: "I want to welcome everybody here to City Hall," he said. "It's the home of Dublin City Council, we've a lot of history here. It's owned by the people of Dublin, and we see no fitter location to welcome some of its more senior citizens. ALONE has played a vital part in this country for elderly people over the past 40 years, and we are proud that it was one of our own, Willie Bermingham – an ex-fireman from the City Council, (or Corporation as it was back then), who established this fabulous charity. ALONE is one of a number of charities that works tirelessly 365 days a year to ensure that our fellow citizens are being looked after."

Speaking on behalf of the people of Dublin, the Lord Mayor thanked everyone involved in ALONE and "most of all the volunteers who work on a daily basis to help some of our older citizens." He continued, "I always maintain that every generation should leave this city in a better place than they found it, but I also maintain that the generations today should acknowledge the work, the hard dedication, which our previous generation have done for us. Too often, we forget in our busy lives that we have many challenges in this city, and many older people out there contributed to Dublin being in the great condition it is today. Today some of them are struggling with homelessness, with isolation, and many experience difficulties. It's fabulous to see so many volunteers who acknowledge that, accept that, and have taken up, I wouldn't say a burden, but a privilege in helping some of the older citizens."And he added, "My Dad keeps reminding me: 'You'd have nothing without me' – and he doesn't let me forget it." The Lord Mayor went on to say he understands that sometimes people need a helping hand "and the State and we politicians don't often seem to hit the right notes with the right people at the time, but it's fairly well established that the work ALONE does for the more senior citizens in society has made the city, the country, a much better, much more rewarding place. I just want to wish you all the very best for the future. Any support you need from the City Council, from myself, you have it! Looking forward to seeing you in the next 40 years." And his promise of support didn't go unnoticed as everyone made a mental note of it!

Eddie Matthews, the Chairperson of ALONE, then took us back to the beginning, acknowledging the roles of "four of the board of trustee colleagues who have played their part in the ALONE story. Pat Morgan, who's here tonight, Michael Hodgins and Patricia Larkin, and my predecessor as Chair, Aidan Bowers, have given over 120 years to the ALONE cause, and I thank them for that here tonight. It was Isaac Newton who was alleged to have said, 'If I have seen further by standing on the shoulders of giants...' Willie Bermingham was such a giant and a visionary far in advance of his time. He had compassion for his fellow Dubliners, and he met them on a daily basis as a fireman and reached out the hand of friendship to them in an unobtrusive way. While compassionate, I am told, by people who knew him, that he had a terrier-like quality, as he snapped at the heels of bureaucrats and brow-beat them into addressing the needs of older persons. I'd like to think that Willie would have approved of how his legacy and vision continues to be honoured in 2017. I should also say that while I mention Willie had a persistent doggedness about him that enabled him to get things done, I think we can all rest easy as the current CEO Seán Moynihan has these very same characteristics in abundance, as witnessed recently by his team!"

Eddie went on to say that he would be watching developments regarding older people with great interest as he had just collected his own free travel pass.

The late founder of ALONE, Willie Bermingham was a fireman so it was fitting that the Chief Fire Officer of Dublin Fire Brigade, Pat Fleming, addressed the audience and remembered Willie who, he said, "displayed the normal firefighter traits of compassion and desire to do good for others. However, as a result of the people and conditions he observed during his work, he went one step further. He decided to do something about it. That took both courage and fortitude. Sometimes, we talk about a person's legacy in life, and Willie has left a wonderful legacy. Something that continues, after his death, and is bigger and has a wider range of services while at the same time, adhering to the same values and beliefs that Willie had. I'm delighted to say that the relationship between ALONE and Dublin Fire Brigade continues today. He is held in great regard by the people in Dublin Fire Brigade who worked with him, but also, in particular, for all the stories that have been passed down about his exploits both within the brigade and also the work that he did in ALONE."

Then Pat made a very important announcement: Dublin Fire Brigade would sign its first ever partnership agreement. It would be with ALONE, in relation to community fire safety. "The purpose of this agreement is to provide enhanced assistance to people at risk, for the mutual benefit of both organisations. As part of this agreement, Dublin Fire Brigade will provide fire safety training for ALONE volunteers and will also refer individuals to ALONE services where appropriate. This is a new initiative, as Dublin Fire Brigade utilises partnership arrangements to further fire safety in vulnerable communities. I think that's probably the future of the fire service in many ways. It's funny that we are following on something that Willie saw as natural 40 years ago – and that is the work of partnerships in the community and linking the official organisation and the community partnerships in order to deliver a service that the official organisation would never be in a position to do."

"That, I think, is a legacy of Willie's that he thought about, but that never came to fruition in the way that we are going to do it today, so I cannot think of a better organisation to begin this process with." Pat continued, "All of us in this country know how much society relies on the work of volunteers, and we also know the huge volume of work that volunteers do, and the huge amount of work that the organisers of these organisations do in facilitating volunteers and making sure that they can give in a way that is beneficial to both the volunteer and the receiver of the service."

Pat also paid tribute to the organisers of ALONE who, he said "took on the mantle of responsibility after Willie's demise and turned ALONE into the organisation that it is today. I won't be here for the second 40th, but somebody will be. I hope the relationship with Dublin Fire Brigade will have deepened and matured within that time."

"This is a party!" Seán Moynihan, Chief Executive of ALONE, reminded the gathering as he thanked the older people who had come along. "You are the reason we exist," he told them, "and we've always been here to promote people's independence, and to provide people with support to make decisions for themselves. It's a great privilege to be here and to have the opportunity to speak on behalf of so many people who have used our services over 40 years. I think together we've shared great happiness and some great sadness as well. We remember all those who have used their services, and the older people who have come to ALONE and the senior citizens of this city who at times need a helping hand."

He went on to acknowledge the Bermingham family and the Larkin family, who wererepresenting Willie's family. "You're really welcome and we're delighted that you're here tonight. I was talking to family members earlier – sometimes they feel it [Willie's death] is so close, and sometimes so far away. My own father died in 1990 as well and it sort of feels that way too." Seán went back to the beginning and remembered the year ALONE was founded, 1977. "So, what else happened in 1977?" He asked. "Well, Red Rum won the Grand National, Jack Lynch became Taoiseach (and we might be about to change Taoiseach again!). Star Wars came out, and we're still watching it, and I made my First Communion! But, I think, Willie founding ALONE was a little more important. I think the great thing that Willie taught us – he saw the issues, and as Pat Fleming put it, he did something about it. There are always excuses about why something couldn't be done. You can see that when crises arise. People say, 'Oh, we can't do this because. . .we can't do that because. . .', and the reality is that there are a lot more reasons why we should do them.

Willie saw older people living in poor housing and poor conditions and as a proud member of the Fire Brigade, he decided to do something about it. I think the real lesson was the proof that one person can change things. And very quickly, what he gathered around him were like-minded individuals, and together they changed lives. They also changed some laws, and ultimately we built on them." Seán also touched on the establishment of the Millennium Plot in Glasnevin cemetery which is owned by ALONE. "Willie saw that people were still being buried in paupers' graves, people being buried in unmarked graves in the early morning, because their families had no money to bury them properly. We know now that that was so wrong, and as Eddie said, by going after bureaucracy, and basically pushing, and influencing, we still use the plot today. Anybody who is unclaimed today still gets buried in that plot, and what we do is we maintain it, we put their names up, and we make sure they are known and remembered. Such a basic thing, to be looked after in life and even in death."

He also paid tribute to the early volunteers and told the guests, "There was a book and we have it in the office – it's a hardback book – and to become a volunteer you had to just sign the book. There was no training like you have these days, you just signed the book. By the time I arrived there were still a good bunch of volunteers and it's great to see so many of them here tonight. I joined in 2008 and it was like taking over managing a football team, there was great promises of money and time to grow and all that, and the week after I started, Lehman Brothers went bust and that was the end of the money, and the work started coming thick and fast! I also turned 40 the same week, so it was a big week and it has been an honour ever since. I'd like to thank the Board because of what happened in 2008, when the money disappeared. The Board made a conscious decision that now was the time that ALONE needed to push out, now was the time to grow, to be there when people needed you, when so much else was going wrong for people."

"What we do is – the services provided by the state are there, the needs of the people are there…we operate in that gap," he continued. "When that gap shifts and moves, we move with it. The future for ALONE is bright. At the moment the good news for both young and old is we're all living longer, and it's a great thing. We rejoice in the skills and abilities of a lot of older people." But, he said, "There's a slight difference between now and 1977. Willie and the volunteers responded to a crisis – we're going to try and prevent it getting to that point. We've a huge homeless crisis in the city, but every house we have, we've 20 applicants." ALONE has expanded, he said, "we now have 600 volunteers, and the plan over the next five years is to spread across the country."

The Real People!

The speeches over, it was the turn of the 'real' people, the guests and volunteers who took to the stage to talk about their own experiences with ALONE. ALONE's oldest volunteer, 90-year-old Sr. Mary Dempsey, enthralled the audience with her experiences of visiting an older man who kept telling her to "go away!", and never taking "no" for an answer.

Volunteer Jeremy Chapman expanded on his belief that some older people are being forced into nursing homes way before their time. And Leo Kelly, who has been befriended by ALONE for over five years, spoke eloquently about isolation and how easily it can happen. You can read the full stories of these three people elsewhere in the book. Perhaps the highlight of this part of the night was Ann McAuley who told her story with frankness and kindness. Ann had been happily married for 56 years when she lost her husband, Gerald, in 2014. Just before that, in 2012, Ann also lost her son, Kevin.

Although Ann has a close relationship with her children, her three daughters live abroad and her son lives a few hours drive away. Enter the window cleaner! One day she was having her windows cleaned when he told her about ALONE's befriending service and offered to get her some literature about it. The next day she called ALONE, "To this day I still tell people it's the best phone call I've ever made," she said. Ann was matched with Colette through the befriending service, and the pair get on like a house on fire. It was a lovely tribute when Ann told the gathering that it was actually her late husband's birthday and she received a warm, supportive round of applause.

There was plenty of time for chatting, eating, cutting the cake, meeting new friends and exchanging phone numbers. People made plans to link up, to meet for coffee, to set the world to rights. But, as we said our goodbyes, there was a certain sadness, wondering what the next forty years will hold for ALONE and, indeed, whether it will be as necessary then as it is now. It all comes down to people like ourselves, human nature, good intentions and the terrier-like approach to government structures adopted by ALONE for the first forty years. See you in 2057!

*   *   *   *

Among the Guests...
Brendan Batt grew up in Terenure and is a great film buff but he was unlucky enough to lose his eyesight five years ago. He was accompanied by one of his carers, Marie Mounsey, who has helped to look after Brendan for the past seven years. Brendan has been visited by ALONE volunteers and really enjoys their company.

Supporting ALONE

There are a number of ways people can support ALONE. Volunteers are the backbone of the organisation. Without them, ALONE would not have existed, and would not continue to exist.

To get involved, you can:

- Volunteer as a Befriender
- Volunteer in the Small Events team
- Organise a volunteer housing maintenance day
- Hold a fundraising event
- Donate to ALONE

ALONE

Thank you

A huge thank you to all involved in the writing and publishing of this book, the older people, former and current volunteers, ALONE staff members, and photographers.

CONTACT DETAILS

ALONE,

Olympic House,

Pleasants Street,

Dublin 8

Telephone: 01 679 1032

Email: hello@alone.ie

Supporting ALONE:

To donate, or for more information, please visit

www.alone.ie

Connect with us on

Facebook   Twitter   Instagram